Redeeming How We Talk

DISCOVER HOW COMMUNICATION FUELS OUR GROWTH, SHAPES OUR RELATIONSHIPS, AND CHANGES OUR LIVES

Ken Wytsma and A. J. Swoboda

MOODY PUBLISHERS

CHICAGO

Some names and details have been changed to protect the privacy of individuals.

Taken from the Holy Bible, New International Version®, NIV®. Copyright © 1973, 1978, 1984, 2011 by Biblica Inc.® Used by permission. All rights reserved worldwide.

Scripture quotations marked ESV are from the ESV® Bible (The Holy Bible, English Standard Version®), copyright © 2001 by Crossway, a publishing ministry of Good News Publishers. Used by permission. All rights reserved.

Scripture quotations marked NASB are taken from the New American Standard Bible®. © Copyright The Lockman Foundation 1960, 1962, 1963, 1968, 1971, 1972, 1973, 1975, 1977, 1995. Used by permission. (www.Lockman.org).

Scripture quotations marked NLV are taken from the Holy Bible, New Life Version. Copyright © 1969–2003 by Christian Literature International, P.O. Box 777, Canby, OR 97013. Used by permission.

Scripture quotations marked NLT are taken from the Holy Bible, New Living Translation, copyright © 1996, 2004, 2007, 2013, 2015 by Tyndale House Foundation. Used by permission of Tyndale House Publishers Inc., Carol Stream, Illinois 60188. All rights reserved.

All emphasis in Scripture has been added.

Edited by Matthew Boffey
Interior design: Ragont Design
Cover design: Connie Gabbert Design and Illustration
Ken Wytsma photo: Benjamin Edwards

Library of Congress Cataloging-in-Publication Data

Names: Swoboda, A. J., 1981- author.
Title: Redeeming how we talk : discover how communication fuels our growth, shapes our relationships, and changes our lives / by A.J. Swoboda & Ken Wytsma.
Description: Chicago : Moody Publishers, 2018. | Includes bibliographical references.
Identifiers: LCCN 2018004416 (print) | LCCN 2018016008 (ebook) | ISBN 9780802496201 (ebook) | ISBN 9780802416179
Subjects: LCSH: Oral communication--Religious aspects--Christianity.
Classification: LCC BV4597.53.C64 (ebook) | LCC BV4597.53.C64 S96 2018 (print) | DDC 241/.672--dc23
LC record available at https://lccn.loc.gov/2018004416

We hope you enjoy this book from Moody Publishers. Our goal is to provide high-quality, thought-provoking books and products that connect truth to your real needs and challenges. For more information on other books and products written and produced from a biblical perspective, go to www.moodypublishers.com or write to:

Moody Publishers
820 N. LaSalle Boulevard
Chicago, IL 60610

1 3 5 7 9 10 8 6 4 2

Printed in the United States of America

We all crave connection. But ironically, we don't spend a lot of time thinking about, or praying about, how our words and our other conversational tools work to draw us close to one another or to God. We are all familiar with the psalm that pleads, "May these words of my mouth and this meditation of my heart be pleasing in your sight, LORD, my Rock and my Redeemer." *Redeeming How We Talk* breaks down how to do just that.

LINDSEY NOBLES
Strategist and Chief Operating Officer at IF:Gathering

In a world where we have tribalized ourselves into identity groups of disagreement, true conversation and dialogue are becoming obsolete. We don't have conversations anymore; the dialogue is predetermined and reinforced in the echo chambers of media. A. J. and Ken have given us not only a history of how we got here and a theology of communication, but wisdom and practical guidance in how we talk to one another. It is time for us to leave our polarized islands of finger pointing and truly learn to ask the deeper questions, gain understanding, and yes, speak to one another in a way that reveals the love and wisdom of God. This book will give you the tools to heal our fractured world one conversation at a time.

RICK MCKINLEY
Lead Pastor of Imago Dei Community in Portland, OR
Author of *The Answer to Our Cry*

What comes out of our mouths is a reflection of what's on our hearts. At a time when our discourse has become more coarse and when it's easier to back into corners with our opinions, rather than engaging with those with whom we may disagree, this book offers a way for us to rethink the importance of civil discourse, and humility and openness in communication. This book comes at a right time when perhaps all of us need a fresh reminder to guard our tongues and our hearts in a way that would honor Christ.

JENNY YANG
Vice President of Advocacy and Policy for World Relief

"We have become a people all alone, together," assert Ken Wytsma and A. J. Swoboda in *Redeeming How We Talk*. Mass communication is more like a corporate cacophony. Few are listening, few speak what's worth hearing. We just keep missing each other. Is there hope of recovery from the current crisis? Is there hope for the kind of *communication* that recovers the lost art of *community*? Wytsma and Swoboda blaze a path out of all the noise that moves toward honest, thoughtful communication where we can listen, hear, and thoughtfully respond.

JERRY ROOT
Professor, Wheaton College

Words have power. This one simple phrase has shaped my adult life in a profound way. There has never been a more important time for a generation to rediscover the power of words than in our current culture. I believe this book invokes a holy understanding of our unique calling as agents of grace, truth, and life in a decaying world.

DANIELLE STRICKLAND
Speaker, author, social justice advocate

It is not just the clarity of their speech that sets Ken and A. J.'s message apart, it is the depth of their listening. This is so much more than a book about words; it is a book that lays open our shouting hearts, and gently questions *why* we speak in the first place. *Redeeming How We Talk* invites us to a more Christlike way to speak, to listen, and to live.

PAUL J. PASTOR
Author of *The Listening Day* devotional series and *The Face of the Deep: Exploring the Mysterious Person of the Holy Spirit*

Not only has civic dialogue become increasingly toxic, we have lost our imagination for how our public discourse could be any different. Fortunately for us, Wytsma and Swoboda have vibrant moral imaginations that they employ to paint a hopeful vision for healthy public communication in a time it is most desperately needed. Moreover, they understand that Jesus Himself offers the way forward, and His kingdom contains all the resources we need to engage in public life free of fear and manipulation, and full of joy and love.

MICHAEL WEAR
Author of *Reclaiming Hope: Lessons Learned in the Obama White House About the Future of Faith in America*

Scripture reminds us that the tongue carries within it the power of life and death. Words matter. They either lift up, or they tear down. In an age of mass communication though, we get overwhelmed with too many words. We don't know which ones to prioritize, and which ones to filter out. In this important work, Ken Wytsma and A. J. Swoboda take us on a journey to recognize the power of words, and to develop a strategy for how to better receive, and pass on, this important currency.

DANIEL HILL
Pastor and author of *White Awake* and *10:10: Life to the Fullest*

Words matter. As Ken Wytsma and A. J. Swoboda suggest, they are "extensions of every heart." If we are to bridge the divides of our time, or simply learn to live together with our deep differences, there is no more important place to start than in redeeming the way we talk. This book is a much-needed reflection on speaking, listening, and living differently in ways that bring healing and reconciliation.

TODD DEATHERAGE
Cofounder, The Telos Group

In this age of the overload of words that are dividing and degrading, I know of no more important topic than *Redeeming How We Talk*. May the church learn to lead by redeeming the gift of communication, that our words would heal and unite humanity, and that our actions would align to the same.

TAMMY DUNAHOO
General Supervisor and V.P. of U.S. Operations, The Foursquare Church

Maybe it's our polarized politics. Or the 24-hour cable news cycle. Or the digital devices that promise to connect us even as they drive us apart. Whatever the reason, it seems like we don't talk anymore. Not really, anyway. We talk past each other, over each other, against each other. In *Redeeming How We Talk*, Wytsma and Swoboda explain how we've come to our current predicament and how we can find our way out. The authors provide a fascinating survey of the history of information and the mechanics of language. Ultimately, they root their prescriptions in the character of a relational God who uses words to create and restore—and calls us to do the same. It's hard to imagine a more timely or important message.

DREW DYCK
Contributing editor at CTPastors.com
Author of *Yawning at Tigers*

Redeeming How We Talk is a striking book. Swoboda and Wytsma have a deep sense of brokenness of modern Western culture and the loneliness and fragmentation that prevail within it. They also are keen readers of Scripture and stir our imaginations with the hope that the Word-made-flesh might indeed be very good news in this cultural milieu. I pray that this book will be read, wrestled with, but most of all, talked about in our churches.

C. CHRISTOPHER SMITH
Founding editor of *The Englewood Review of Books*
Coauthor of *Slow Church*

I am grateful for the work that A.J. And Ken have put in to write such a timely book like this because words light or darkness, life or death. This book teaches us who are the walking letters representing Christ practically how to recognize words of darkness and death and how to use our words to bring both light and life. I hope you read this book and act accordingly so you can spread more of Christ's light and life.

DAVID M. BAILEY
Executive Director of Arrabon
Coauthor of *Race, Class, and The Kingdom of God* Study Series

To Morris Dirks. Thanks for loving me like a son.
And for letting me lean on you like a father.
—A. J.

To Nicholas Wolterstorff, who helped me find my words,
and to Stephan Bauman, who helped me share them with the world.
—Ken

Civilization is constituted by reasoned conversation. . . . Civilized peoples are able to reason with one another; barbarians club one another.

MICHAEL NOVAK

Contents

Introduction: When Language Gets Lost   13

PART 1: THE WORLD OF WORDS

1. A Creative Word   21
2. Propaganda   35
3. The Challenge of Connecting in a Digital Age   51
4. A Brief History of Information   67
5. Here Be Dragons   81

PART 2: THE WORDS OF GOD

6. Jesus Speaks   99
7. What Is Godly Speech?   111
8. On Wisdom and Words   131
9. The Mechanics of Hearing One Another   143
10. The Unity of the Church   157
11. The Art of Winning People Back   169
12. To Speak a Better Word   183

Conclusion: Blessed Words   203
Acknowledgments   211
Notes   213
About the Authors   221

Introduction

When Language Gets Lost

In 1970s San Francisco, an unknown man walks from his home to the Golden Gate Bridge. His mission is simple: to jump. Passing person after person, tourist after tourist, business owner after business owner, the man climbs the bridge's four-foot safety railing. He jumps, falling 220 feet to his death.

During the course of the ensuing investigation, the man's psychiatrist, along with the assistant medical examiner, discovered a note on his bureau. It read:

> I'm going to walk to the bridge. If one person smiles at me on the way, I will not jump.[1]

The image is so stark: a man walking to his death, the San Franciscans around him unaware of the lifesaving mercy they can show with the simplest of gestures. And if a single stranger's smile could have saved this man's life, what might a single word of kindness have done?

We have become a world of people all alone, together.[2]

Humans are relational beings. Handcrafted and honed by a

brilliant, relational Maker, we are made to reflect His relational qualities. As such, we have been given power—the power to build bridges or build walls. Through our lives and interactions, each of us wields social influence and power that are rarely considered, barely understood, and often underappreciated.

Our lives, smiles—and yes, *words*—have power. Words can begin a war. Words can end a war. Words on a page can inspire a lunatic's genocide. And words can begin a process of great healing. Words can fell a relationship or reconcile one that has long gone cold. Words can terrorize, and words can bear the gospel of peace.

How much time do we spend thinking and praying about how our words shape our lives? Not nearly as much as the time we spend using them.

Communication is one of the main ways we exemplify our humanity. And we are endowed with a variety of means to do so—a mouth, hands, facial muscles, and body posture. Whether through looks, words, gestures, or pictures, we all communicate. Even silence can speak louder than words. Whether it's face-to-face, in a crowded restaurant, or online, we converse with others constantly.

Without communication, we wither away. Solitary confinement—the cruelest form of imprisonment—isn't merely confinement to a physical space; it cuts off human communication and relationship. If human touch is withheld from babies during their earliest stages of formation, there is a greater chance they will die—even if they are properly nourished.[3] And research reveals that suicide rates skyrocket among those who are disconnected from friends, family, and even church.[4] We need other humans. Communication is what makes our relationships possible. Even the simple, nonverbal communication of a smile can be a matter of life and death in this world.

In recent decades a puzzle has presented itself. While the ability to communicate with one another is far easier now than at any point in human history, we are—more and more—experiencing the dark pangs of loneliness and isolation. The *volume* of communication is not bringing joy or meaning to life. We can gather information, share ideas, spread opinions, and disseminate lies quicker and easier than ever, all by virtue of electronic and virtual communication. We can Google information about a coming concert while texting a friend on the other side of the country and listening to a podcast. Though we may have incredible ways of communicating, we rarely know *how* to talk with one another. Though we communicate, we do not necessarily converse.

The conversational atrophy brought on by information overload is bearing demonstrable consequences on the fabric of human society. After the 2016 election, it was discovered that 47 percent of those who voted for Hillary Clinton did not have one close relationship with someone who voted for Donald Trump. Similarly, some 31 percent of Donald Trump supporters had no close friends who supported Hillary Clinton.[5] We have become a culture of walls, not a culture of bridges. The political left and right no longer dialogue with each other.

Such information overload has, in turn, led to a breakdown in religious communities. Different generations increasingly look skeptically upon one another. Instead of talking *with*, we talk over or about, and though God is always building unity among His children, we seem to be increasingly working against Him.

The ability of humans to talk in dignified and respectful ways has fallen on hard times as well. It isn't that the amount of information or words has declined, but rather that deep, transformative, and redemptive communication has fallen victim to the new realities of modern culture. Whatever the cause—maybe the internet, social media, television, or simply the pace of contemporary society—we are losing our ability to connect with one another. The Christian intellectual Os Guinness once wrote, "The outcome of instant, total information is inflation—when more and more of anything is available, less and less is valuable."[6]

Question

More than ever in our world of endless information, we must ask the deeper questions: Why has God given us the ability to communicate? Why do words have power? How does God expect us to use the gifts of speech and communication? How is communication in modern life transforming our use of words?

Forgetting How to Talk

We speak all day but rarely think about the words we say. I (Ken) realized this on a recent trip to the Netherlands with my dad and two of my daughters.

I lived in the Netherlands between the ages of three and seven because my father had been stationed there with the Navy. These early childhood years are some of the most formative for learning a language, and I became fluent in Dutch. In fact, I became *too* fluent—or at least my parents thought so. Fearing I would lose some of my native tongue, they transferred me from a Dutch school to an English-speaking one. And when we returned to the States, I wasn't allowed to speak Dutch, only English, so that I could catch up with my peers.

I distinctly remember the day my dad spoke Dutch to me again after two years of living stateside. I had absolutely no idea what he was saying. My ability to speak the language fluently and intuitively had vanished quicker than it had come.

Language is a lot like a muscle. Use it and it becomes stronger. Neglect it and it atrophies. To this day, I give my dad a hard time for having me speak only English during those years. I'm one of the few people I know who *was* bilingual but is no longer. I lost a language.

So on my recent trip back to Holland with my dad and daughters, I found it strange to experience the language. I was able to make many of the unique Dutch sounds and say just about any word (even a word I was told the Dutch used to root out German spies during World War II—because Germans couldn't pronounce it correctly even if they spoke Dutch). I also felt a strange comfort around this language—almost as if it wasn't foreign but instead familiar, though I couldn't understand what was being said.

In similar ways, with the accumulation of words in our contemporary world, I suspect we have begun to lose the language or spiritual understanding of what God intended when He gave us speech. Maybe we're awash in the material of conversation but not truly connecting with others. Maybe we've lost a language or at least the ability to use words well and respect their power.

More often than not, we don't realize the power of our words to shape those around us. As followers of Jesus, we need to recognize that words will shape our environment. Our words have spiritual power. They change our reality and work in tandem with our actions.

Words are central to the calling of Christian faith, ministry, and witness. With words we write, preach, and teach. With words we lead, motivate, and inspire. With words we love God and our neighbor. In an age of fractured relationships, loving words and godly communication are how we mend our broken bonds.

In the pages that follow, we'll synthesize theology and philosophy, and we'll even offer a bit of self-help, to reclaim the holiness of human speech and the relevance of meaningful conversation for life today. In short, we'll explore the conversational ethics of the Bible. We'll look at what God says about our words and consider how we, as Christians, can use them to engage in rich, nourishing conversations that echo the voice of God and speak life into His world.

To renew our conversational habits, we must relearn the nature, purpose, and practice of godly speech. Only then can we be fully human, honor our Creator, and get closer to the deep relationships we all desire.

Will you join us in this conversation?

Part 1

THE WORLD
OF WORDS

Civil discourse isn't the answer to everything, but uncivil discourse isn't the answer to anything.

N. T. WRIGHT

Chapter 1

A Creative Word

*Nature is the one song
of praise that never stops singing.*

RICHARD ROHR

We hope it never comes to this.

But if, during the course of your life, you find yourself held hostage, crisis negotiators say there is one thing you can do that may very well save your life. And it isn't necessarily to disarm your captor.

Your best bet is to talk about the weather.

Or your child. Or your job. Or your favorite band.

This may seem like an odd or even silly piece of advice, but time and again, professionals have seen people survive hostage situations through the simple act of small talk.

This is because conversation personalizes and dignifies us. People are far more likely to kill or harm what they perceive as an *object* rather than a *person*. Objects don't make small talk or chit-chat. Objects do not talk. Objects, such as rocks and paper clips and orange peels, just sit there quietly and have no feelings, no breath, no story. But *people* talk.

Our ability to speak with power and intention is one of God's richest gifts. Without words, how else would we resolve our conflicts? God gave us words so that we would not have to turn to violence. The richness of language is God's way of giving us tools to resolve our human relationships and also to be vulnerable and honest with Him. Words are an essential part of our humanity and what it means to be made in the likeness of God. They enable us to not only avoid or resolve conflict but also to bless God, bless our neighbor, communicate our feelings, sing our praises, and shout our joy.

If we are to study the biblical importance of words, we must look at the first words—God's. His speech is the beginning and end of a theology of words.

God Talks

The first thing God does in the entire Bible is *speak*:

> In the beginning, God created the heavens and the earth. . . . *And God said*, "Let there be light." (Gen. 1:1, 3)

So begins Scripture's story of God and creation. Within the very first verse of the Holy Scriptures are three critical components of the nature of words.

First, and most importantly, God's words are fundamentally creative in nature. What is God's first act in the Bible? God *said*. He talked. Words were spoken. And what was the result of God speaking these first words? Light. The result of a word from God was all the light the world has ever needed.

But God does not stop there—God continues speaking. As a result of His continued speaking, the vault is created to separate the waters. Then the dry ground and the water in the air. Then vegetables and trees. Then the moon and the sun. Then the stars. Then the fish and the birds. Then the beasts of the land. Then *humanity*.

Each movement of creation begins demonstrably with a simple "And God said . . ." The lingering message conveyed by this rhythm is that God does not create the world with slaves, angels, subcontractors, or even His hands.[1] God creates the whole wide world with nothing more than His words. We live in a *spoken* world. All the created universe that one can see, taste, touch, and smell is created in one single chapter by a few words from God.

Words are in and of themselves *creative*. God does not ramble some magic formula or make a massive inspirational speech to a creation that already existed and just needed a little direction. There was nothing. Then there were words. Then there was everything.

The simplicity of this action demonstrates the power of God and the nature of words: they are paramount to existence. There is no such thing as an empty or harmless word. Speech is always powerful—whether it builds up, distorts, or tears down. Everything in the world is the result of words. It began with a series of words.

But the opposite is also true. Words can undermine all the good things that God has begun. This is precisely why the Hebrew tradition tells us, "The tongue has the power of life and death" (Prov. 18:21). Words can create and, as we will see, destroy.

Molecular physicists have theorized that every atom—if we could see it at its most basic level—is a vibration. In his book *The Elegant Universe*, Brian Greene suggests that, simply yet scientifically speaking, matter is music.[2] Biblically speaking, all matter is actually embodied sound—what Christians might describe as the

There was **NOTHING.**

Then there were **WORDS.**

Then there was **EVERYTHING.**

words of God. God *spoke* the world into existence. In one sense the universe is God's voice in physical form.

The second thing we notice about the nature of words is that all of this is done *with just a few* words.

In our own culture the assumption is often that we need *more* words to get things done. Edward Everett was the keynote speaker at the dedication of the Gettysburg National Cemetery. He talked for over two hours. Immediately afterward, and so quickly that photographers didn't even get a good picture, Abraham Lincoln delivered his Gettysburg Address. It was a simple 272 words, and it took no more than two minutes.

God created everything with a few words. Likewise, Lincoln summarized the struggle of the whole Civil War. This speaks to the value of intentionality, not the number, of our words. We need intentional words, not more words themselves. Words are creative, even when they are few.

"Let your words be few," the author of Ecclesiastes writes (Eccl. 5:2), and later, "Of making many books there is no end" (12:12). That has not been the habit of human beings. Jesus even tells us that we will "give account" for every word we speak (Matt. 12:36). James counsels us that "everyone should be quick to listen, slow to speak and slow to become angry" (James 1:19). Even Jesus chastised the Pharisees for thinking their prayers would be answered because of their many, rather than humble, words. Where we tend to multiply words, God opts for a few creative ones.

The third and final thing we'd like to point out is how words themselves have the power to liberate and set others free. God's creative words not only made and animated us as humans, but they created freedom and space for us to live into our full humanity.

God's plan is, in the phrase of our friend Wynand de Kock, "to make space for life."[3] In the narrative of God speaking in Genesis, we hear a phrase repeated over and over: "Let there be . . ."

God's creative process has been a point of great discussion among biblical and theological scholars.[4] The famed Karl Barth argued that "Let there be . . ." speaks to God's great patience. While God created with His words and spoke the "Let there be," He still creates capacity for species and creation to change, grow, and reproduce. No other creation account depicts a God who extends this kind of freedom and generativity to what has been made. God creates the birds and the trees and the people to have freedom and be able to create—to have offspring, flourish, and, in Adam's case, even name creation. The present world is the result of God "letting" things flourish and develop in their own creative ways. "Let there be . . ." is not only a mandate; it's an invitation. God is no micromanager; His words extend creative freedom to His creation.

The Devil Talks

God creates the world with just a few words. Likewise, Satan mars the whole world with just a few words.

Somewhere along the way—Scripture doesn't specify when—one of God's greatest angels, Lucifer, rebelled against Him. Also known as Satan, Lucifer is a created being. He is not an eternal being. There was a time when Satan was not. As with the rest of creation, God made Lucifer.

Because Satan is a created being, his finitude limits his powers. He does not have the power and authority that God does. For instance, Satan is not omnipresent as God is—he is not everywhere all the time. Satan is not omniscient—he has no foreknowledge of all events that are to come. He is not all-powerful. In fact, he is bound to submit to God's final word, as evidenced by his conversation with God in the first chapter of Job. Yet while Satan lacks God's eternal qualities, he has rational power to subvert God's works.

Still, how does the devil get his work done? More than anything, he uses words. In fact, it is through words that the devil does his "finest" work. He is so good at using words that he is called *Satan*, meaning "accuser." Not only does the devil use to destroy what God uses to create—words—but he is literally named for what he does with them.

So just as God created the world with words, the devil manipulates the world with words. Some of God's first words of instruction to Adam and Eve have to do with food: "You are free to eat from any tree in the garden; but you must not eat from the tree of the knowledge of good and evil" (Gen. 2:16–17). Adam and Eve were free to eat from any tree *except* one.

Enter Satan, pouncing on Eve. The very first words out of the snake's mouth in Genesis are framed as a deconstructive question: "Did God really say, 'You must not eat from any tree in the garden'?" (Gen. 3:1). The devil's work in the world—his destructive activity of stealing, robbing, and confusing—begins with words, specifically with a cynical question. In a tricky and maligning way, the very good word of God that made the world is being questioned. God begins a creative kingdom with words, whereas the devil begins a destructive kingdom with words.

"Did God really say . . . ?" the devil asks. The big problem in the garden is that God's word is quickly forgotten and replaced with Satan's question. This is immediately reflected in Eve's attempt to explain God's command to Satan during her temptation:

"But God did say, 'You must not eat fruit from the tree that is in the middle of the garden, and you must not *touch* it, or you will die" (Gen. 3:3). Eve, in that critical moment, reveals humanity's vexing and perennial problem: an inability to remember what God actually said. Of course, God never once commanded Adam or Eve not to *touch* the tree. Rather, God commanded them not to *eat* from the tree. Eve added to God's word, indicating that she had forgotten it.

The problem is not just that she forgot a line verbatim or did not commit it to memory. The passage reveals that she perhaps never understood the heart of it, or didn't understand why it was important to fully obey God's command. It's when we don't understand or trust God's heart, beautiful design, and goodness that we begin to question His commands and then subsequently disobey.

The devil is a wordsmith and a master of spin. Making things more challenging, the devil actually speaks truth at times. Later in Scripture, when Satan tempts Jesus in the desert, we find that he has a working knowledge of the Bible. He quotes Scripture to Jesus. Satan knows the truth, but he misuses it with evil motives— to manipulate and control rather than to set people free. Satan knows how to take God's good and creative word and then use it for his own purposes.

Once Satan's word is obeyed in the garden, the relationships there begin to fall apart. Adam and Eve blame each other for what has happened. The breakdown in human relationships becomes more and more pronounced as the Genesis narrative continues. Within even a few chapters, we see the first instance of murder and the subjugation of women in the practice of polygamy.

Dietrich Bonhoeffer framed Satan's use of the truth like this:

> There is a truth which is of Satan. Its essence is that under the
> semblance of truth it denies everything that is real. It lives
> upon hatred of the real and of the world which is created and
> loved by God. . . . God's truth judges created things out of
> love, and Satan's truth judges them out of envy and hatred.
> God's truth has become flesh in the world and is alive in the
> real, but Satan's truth is the death of all reality.[5]

The fall of humankind didn't begin by eating the wrong fruit, but
by an uncritical dialogue with the devil.

To show the evolving picture of a humanity spiraling farther
and farther away from Eden, the biblical text employs the image of
"going east." After they are cast out from the garden, Adam and Eve
go to the "east side of the Garden of Eden" (Gen. 3:24). Cain, the
child of Adam and Eve, is sent farther east to the land of Nod after
murdering his brother Abel (Gen. 4:16). Then humanity travels
even farther east to the land of Shinar, where they build the Tower
of Babel (Gen. 11:1–4). East, east, and farther east. Humanity wan-
ders away from the land God had established. It is not until God
invites Abram to go the Promised Land that the return west begins.

The lesson? Listening to the words of Satan displaces humanity from the will of God.

As those in the world listen to the word of Satan—a habit
begun with Adam and Eve—human relationships fall apart. Conversation becomes increasingly difficult. This is seen in the story
of Babel. As humanity gives in to full-fledged idolatry and attempts to build a tower to heaven, God curses them with a divided
tongue. Listening to Satan leads to idolatry and the breakdown
of relationships, further leading to the breakdown of civil, human
discourse. It's a tragic cycle.

We Become What We Hear

We can see from examining how God uses words that their main purposes—at least in the creation account—are to create, free, and establish. However, when we look at the way Satan uses words, we see he has the opposite intent—to divide, hurt, marginalize, and deconstruct. Whatever God does with words, Satan tries to undo with words. This is why Satan is called the Father of Lies.

This contrast frames one of Jesus' more famous indictments of the Pharisees in Scripture when He likened Himself to a Good Shepherd and implicated them as false shepherds or thieves who come to kill and destroy.

In John 10, Jesus said:

> Truly, truly, I say to you, I am the door of the sheep. All who came before Me are thieves and robbers, but the sheep did not hear them. I am the door; if anyone enters through Me, he will be saved, and will go in and out and find pasture. *The thief comes only to steal and kill and destroy; I came that they may have life, and have it abundantly.* (vv. 7–10 NASB)

If God's will is for an abundantly good creation, and evil works to bend and destroy it, the obvious question is: upon whose words will we build our lives?

In Matthew 7:24–27, Jesus tells a parable of two ways to build a house. You can either build your house on the words of Jesus—pictured as building on the stable rock—or you can hear the words of Jesus but choose to not build on them—described as building on sand. "Everyone who hears these words of mine and *puts them into practice* is like a wise man who built his house on the rock," Jesus said.

Do we build our lives and identities around what Jesus speaks over us? Do we sit in that reality and let it shape us? We can encourage one another to choose the stability of Christ over the shakiness of culture. We can choose to influence our family and friends and to find voices who will similarly speak wise words into our lives. We can do so much better than letting the devil's words of spin and destruction set the framework for how we live our lives.

We all build our lives on words. We either build our lives around words that are trustworthy, true, and resonant, or we build our lives on words that are deceptive, lacking, or hollow. Our lives are built or broken by the words we believe.

This is why theology is drastically important. Theology, the study of God, becomes paramount to living faithfully in relationship with God. Karl Barth once remarked, "In the church of Jesus Christ there can and should be no non-theologians."[6] While in its worst case, theology can be just bickering about words, Barth was pointing out the reality that thinking through the words we use to talk about God is central to the task of following Jesus. This is true for everyone, not just academics, since it so profoundly shapes how we understand God, and thus how we live. This is why we have had creeds—statements (words)—that articulate something of the nature of God. The Christian church spends so much time thinking about its words because they greatly shape who we become.

The preacher Will Willimon tells the story of a student who got into an argument with an Orthodox priest. When the student said he did not believe the creed, the priest responded, "Well, you just say it. It's not that hard to master. With a little effort, most can quickly learn it by heart." The student then retorted, not confident his dilemma was understood. His issue was that he didn't *believe* certain elements of the creed, such as the virgin birth. Recitation wasn't the issue.

Or so he thought. The priest reiterated, "You just say it. Particularly when you have difficulty believing it, you just keep saying it. It will come to you eventually."[7] This references a deep formational reality: we eventually become our words.

We not only become the words we believe about God, but we also become the words spoken over us by ourselves, others, and society.

A young man we know tells a story. He has dreams and desires—many of which are in his reach—to become an artist. Yet, every time he gets close to living these dreams, he makes some decision that ultimately undermines what he wants to do. He keeps pulling the rug out from under his own feet.

He remembers as a child telling his father his dream, only to be shut down. "Get realistic," his dad told him. "Do you really think you can do that with your life? How will you make money?" Even though he has long been out of his parents' home, every time he gets close to his dream, he is subtly compelled to sabotage it. Because of the doubt and objection instilled by one person who spoke words of futility over him, he has given up his pursuit of the vocation to which God has called him.

The power that words have to shape our identity at an early age is well attested. It's common to hear testimonies of people whose growth was stilted by critical words. Conversely, we know stories of boys and girls who dared to become who they are because of encouraging words spoken by a teacher, celebrity, or sports figure at just the right moment.

When we realize the potential of words for good, we can find the motivation we need to improve our relationships, families, and communities simply by rethinking *how* we talk. The right words can free us to define our circumstances, and we can set others free by the words we speak over them. Even our small talk has the power to save the lives of hostages. This is why we must attend relentlessly to the words we speak over others.

God made the world with words, and He made words powerful. The devil seeks to destroy the world with words, and his words are powerful too. The first great lesson in redeeming how we talk is deciding whose words we will listen to. They are the words we will build our lives on and the words we will echo to others.

Chapter 2

Propaganda

Studies of propaganda are, in the most general sense, studies of language and its use in the public domain. Language, whether in the form of messaging, mythology, poetry, metaphor, or even imagery, conforms to culture.

AARON FRY

If we were to look up any photo of Saddam Hussein, the ruthless former dictator of Iraq, we would find a litany of pictures of the warlord smiling. Saddam always smiled for the camera. Why?

Saddam, like many other despots, did this as a part of a larger effort to control his image, projecting confidence and happiness to cover up the despotic reality beneath. Saddam's smiling photos were just one of many instances of what we all know as *propaganda*.

Propaganda has been around for nearly as long as there has been documented history. The ancients used images and disinformation to enlist support from the masses. We see this when Nero, the emperor of Rome, pins the blame for the burning of his city on Christians as a way to turn support away from the newly formed religious community.[1]

While propaganda—as a means to an end—is identifiable, the word itself didn't officially come into being until Pope Gregory XV created the *Sacra Congregatio de Propaganda Fide*, or Sacred Congregation for the Propagation of the Faith. This was a Vatican organization, and its purpose is reflected in its name: to propagate—or spread—Roman Catholicism.

I (Ken) first learned of the interesting origin of the word *propaganda* when, walking through the streets of Rome, I saw its Latin inscription over one of the old buildings built and used by the *Sacra Congregatio*. The Latin word *propaganda* in large letters was hard to miss and seemed strangely out of place.

From this rather inauspicious, religious beginning, the word eventually morphed into its modern meaning: methods and techniques of persuasion by an authoritative institution.

It was during World War I that *propaganda* reached new heights. Mark Crispin Miller, as quoted in Tim Wu's *The Attention Merchants*, writes, "It was not until 1915 that governments first systematically deployed the entire range of modern media to rouse their population to fanatical assent." Wu comments, "The entry of the State into the game—with its vast resources and monopoly on force—would be spectacularly consequential."[2]

It was Lord Kitchener, the famous British commander, who first used propaganda as a strategic government tool to quickly provide the British army with recruits at the outset of World War I. Lord Kitchener used posters, which had been rapidly developing as an art form under French artists of the day. "And thus began the first state-run attention harvest, or what historians would later call the 'first systematic propaganda campaign directed at the civilian population,'" writes Wu.[3]

Upon entering the Great War, the United States borrowed

from the success of Lord Kitchener's publicity campaigns. George Creel, who had helped President Woodrow Wilson win reelection (ironically, under a message of neutrality regarding the war), led these efforts. Creel had a vision for using scientific techniques in order to build "'ardor and enthusiasm' for the war." As Tim Wu writes:

> Wilson, who felt indebted to Creel anyway, was so taken with Creel's idea that, about a week after asking Congress to declare war, he placed Creel in charge of a new "Committee on Public Information," the first institutionalized federal propaganda agency in American history.[4]

Creel's Committee on Public Information (CPI) handled the dissemination of propaganda using the methods available at the time—the heavy artillery of newspapers, magazines, and posters. One of the more successful posters Britain had used was of Lord Kitchener pointing a finger at the viewer, with text exclaiming, "Your Country Needs You." From this came the most successful of the US posters: the iconic Uncle Sam.

Credit: Library of Congress, Prints & Photographs Division, WWI Posters, [LC-DIG-ppmsca-37468; LC-DIG-ppmsc-03521]

The CPI would come to comprise twenty domestic subdivisions, with a staff of 150,000 dedicated solely to shaping public opinion and garnering support for the war effort. They printed 75 million pamphlets and books and reached "a very precisely estimated 134,454,514" men and women with short pro-war messages delivered by volunteers and celebrities.[5] These are staggering numbers, and this propaganda profoundly shaped how Americans thought about national pride, democracy, and our duty to promote democracy in the world. Consider Wilson's declaration of war speech, which contains one of the most influential sentences of the twentieth century: "The world must be made safe for democracy." Through its eloquence and lofty vision, coupled with Creel's propaganda, it left an indelible mark on subsequent generations.

Propaganda changed the American cultural landscape—not only by creating fervor for war in what had previously been an ambivalent and neutral country, but also by creating an anti-German spillover. Prior to the war, German had been the most taught second language in America. The backlash on German culture affected beer sales, led to one town in Ohio killing German breeds of dogs, and arguably played a role in the Prohibition legislation passed shortly after the war, as the vast majority of beer makers in America were of German descent.[6]

Most Americans have had their understanding of the word *propaganda* permanently altered, if not by the legacy of the First World War, then certainly by the legacy of the Nazis in World War II. Our view of German propaganda under Adolph Hitler is one of sinister uses of persuasion and information control. It was Hitler who, ironically, as a World War I veteran himself, wrote a tract from prison praising the brilliant use of the aforementioned and formative British propaganda.[7]

In the online *Oxford Dictionaries*, the primary definition of *propaganda* has moved from its initial religious connotation to one of political strategy. In fact, it now connotes spin; it is "information, especially of a biased or misleading nature, used to promote a political cause or point of view."[8] The spreading of ideas for the promotion of religion morphed into, and was overshadowed by, the distortion of truth for political gain.

Today, college courses on propaganda often concern the topics of literacy, art, or advertising. That propaganda plays a role in consumerism shows how far it's come from its religious roots. It's now nefarious—a tool for manipulation. And, as Jason Stanley sadly wrote, "A society that is deeply affected by propaganda will be one in which certain legitimate routes that an individual's life path can take will be closed off."[9] In other words, propaganda limits us, pigeonholes us, and ultimately leads us down roads we otherwise wouldn't have walked. This is why we must learn to recognize propaganda.

How does propaganda show up in culture today? How do we get tangled up with it, even when we have good motives? How do we resist it? And what are some of the ways we can more actively choose how we're influenced so that we may chart new, better, and more humane paths to walk? These are some of the themes we'll grapple with in the rest of this chapter.

Persuasion

The issue of propaganda brings up a bigger question of persuasion. In everyday life and in the economic and political institutions and systems of our day, how do we interact with the language of sales, marketing, and branding? Even more important, since most of us have platforms via social media, how do we fashion our *own* language and rhetoric? Is it straightforward and honest, or is it propaganda and spin meant to shape how people perceive us and the ideas we care about most deeply?

We can all think of a time when someone tried to sell us something. It raises our inner skeptic. We question motives. We put up our defenses. We don't trust what we're hearing.

In many respects, this is an age-old issue.

In the first century, the apostle Paul had to deal with society's propensity for persuasion and their readiness to migrate in herds to the latest or best idea or powerful person. It seemed that better orators or more dynamic personalities had arrived on the scene in the cosmopolitan city of Corinth, and the Christian community was breaking itself up into factions—some followed Paul and others followed Apollos. It was a pattern the apostle Paul didn't want anything to do with.

We find Paul writing to the Corinthian church, "My message and my preaching were not with wise and persuasive words, but with a demonstration of the Spirit's power" (1 Cor. 2:4). He goes on to say:

> You are still worldly. For since there is jealousy and quarreling among you, are you not worldly? Are you not acting like mere humans? For when one says, "I follow Paul," and another, "I follow Apollos," are you not mere human beings? What, after all, is Apollos? And what is Paul? Only servants, through whom you came to believe—as the Lord has assigned to each his task. I planted the seed, Apollos watered it, but God has been making it grow. So neither the one who

plants nor the one who waters is anything, but only God, who makes things grow. (3:3–7)

Believers were starting to buy the lie that there was power in a particular person. Paul was trying to snap them out of that idea and remind them of the power of the Spirit. They were forming allegiances and becoming blind.

Much of modern social media and advertising are subtle and destructive in that they create something called "confirmation bias." A confirmation bias is when the thing we already believe is affirmed, thus reinforcing our belief. In the final analysis, it is the gathering of hollow evidence to support a conclusion we've already reached.

In marketing, many multinational corporations spend billions of dollars not on "front-end" advertisement (trying to get potential customers to buy their products) but on "back-end" advertisement—convincing customers to be pleased with their purchase. If we're not being persuaded to buy something, we're being assured that we made the best purchase and are now happier for it.

Tim Wu, whom we quoted just a bit ago, has written at great lengths about the effects of constant, ubiquitous advertising on our lives. In *The Attention Merchants* he provides a history of advertising in the US and its escalating nature. Just one generation ago, no one would have expected advertising to so thoroughly saturate our lives. Not only has that happened, but now networks of our friends and families sell us products, and the phones we carry everywhere enable us to sell at any time.

We are reminded of this every time we get on a long domestic flight, when the TV screen on the seatback plays advertisements nonstop unless we purchase DirecTV for the flight. Can you imagine a more helpless position than having your attention hijacked by a constant barrage of marketing for hours on end? But the nooks and crannies of life that advertising has filled today are as ubiquitous and unending. Wu writes, "Bit by bit, what was once shocking became normal, until the shape of our lives yielded further and further to the logic of commerce—but gradually enough that we should now find nothing strange about it."[10]

Our world has descended further into what an exasperated Thoreau decried in the 1800s, long before the emergence of media-driven advertising, when he said, "Let us consider the way in which we spend our lives. This world is a place of business. What an infinite bustle! I am awaked almost every night by the panting of the locomotive. It interrupts my dreams. There is no sabbath."[11]

Social media does this too. Take Facebook, for example. Its algorithms are powerful. They monitor everything you are doing on Facebook—from what you "like" to the amount of time you hover over a video or post. This feedback then shapes the nature of the content Facebook shares in your newsfeed. As this algorithm continually learns about you (e.g., you seem to like political articles that come from a conservative viewpoint), it shows you more and more of that kind of content. The cycle deepens; the more you like posts that fit your mental profile, the more they appear, and the more they form your mental profile.

But if all we see are things that reinforce our value set, we falsely begin to assume that our view is correct, based only on the volume of others saying the same thing. We don't realize the degree to which there are counterarguments, or that our friend is seeing another highly curated newsfeed—just as we are—but with liberal politics.

If all we see agrees with us, we must be right. But all the while, it is our own preferences and engagement, as well as the agendas of others who are trying to sell us something, that shape the news we're reading—not the validity of the content. In many respects, Facebook slowly and subtly leads all of us to our most extreme self. It's classic confirmation bias.

Isn't that both profound and disturbing?

If the atmosphere we're breathing is leading us further and further away from the center and further away from truly being in contact or conversation with other viewpoints, we are losing our ability to interact with diverse opinions and think critically. And as we're losing our ability to talk to or understand one another, we're losing our ability to be in relationship with people whose viewpoints differ from our own.

Advertising culture and language is an impediment to this growth and, at an extreme, stands antithetical to human flourishing and spirituality.

In an instance of calling out nontheologically informed or self-centered desires, Paul writes about the future when people will not want to put up with sound doctrine (the hard work of patterning our minds in theological or just manners) and instead will want their desires placed at the center of conversation as well as education and theological discourse. "For the time will come when people will not put up with sound doctrine. Instead, to suit their own desires, they will gather around them a great number of teachers to say *what their itching ears want to hear*" (2 Tim. 4:3).

Biblical faith calls us to look to others and consider them above ourselves. Selfishness and unbelief cause us to overlook others and obsess on ourselves. Propaganda, then, in the modern sense, does not stand for the propagation of faith but rather the negation of it. Theology—high and true thinking about God—is moved to the periphery in an advertising-saturated culture and in the industrialized squirrel cage of pervasive social media.

Bestselling author Matthew Crawford, in his book *The World beyond Your Head*, writes:

> Attention is the thing that is most one's own: in the normal course of things, we choose what to pay attention to, and in a very real sense this determines what is real for us; what is actually present to our consciousness. Appropriations of our attention are then an especially intimate matter.[12]

It's what we pay attention to most that forms what we most believe. And of course, what we most believe is the beginning of all we do.

Fodder for Words

Most conversations begin with borrowed material—the weather, what movies are currently popular, the latest from *The Walking Dead*, politics, the news, comedy shows, and whatever might be trending online. The inputs significantly inform and steer our outputs.

But the great essayists counseled that we ought to look *inside* ourselves for some of our content. The famous minimalist Thoreau wrote an essay entitled "Life without Principle" in which he spotlighted the foolishness of over-engaging with meaningless information or conversations outside of ourselves at the expense of self-knowledge. He writes, "The person who is always going to the Post Office hasn't heard from himself for a long while."[13]

In many ways, society was unprepared for the propaganda blitz that hit at the beginning of the twentieth century and for the ensuing advertising culture it spawned. Maybe one of our problems with speech—our inattention to wise words and our saturation with foolish ones—has arisen from the new values and uses of communication that have dominated culture and to which we are reacting.

As propaganda has moved from spreading faith to suffocating it, many of the disciplines and practices of our inner lives have atrophied, or, more accurately, are being used idolatrously. How can we be attentive to God's presence and voice if our very capacity for attention is fragmented? How can we worship Him in fullness if our loyalty is constantly diluted by daily allegiance to politics and consumer spending? And how can we engage in life-giving speech and relationship with those different from us if our habits have been persistently malformed by the propaganda machine that is modern culture?

The Resistance

The biblical prophet Micah, a contemporary of Isaiah, Amos, and Hosea, was sent to Judah to warn God's people about a life of exploitative injustice. He told them, "Your rich people are violent; your inhabitants are liars and their tongues speak deceitfully" (Mic. 6:12).

Lies and deceit are the bricks and mortar of unjust systems and societies. Truth is inconvenient in such places, whether in Micah's day or our own. But in the complicated and ever-growing space of communication and persuasion, how can we center our words and speech? How can we resist the temptation to satisfy ourselves through propagandistic words?

One of the more provocative books I (Ken) have read in a

long time is from the Old Testament theologian Walter Brueggemann. Brueggemann has long been known for writing books against what he calls the Empire (any institution that sets itself up as the definer of reality) and calling us to a prophetic imagination. A prophetic imagination, like the prophets of old, invites us to envision a higher and more just way, give a voice to truth, and issue a strong call for society to walk justly and pursue what's right.

One of his more recent books that had a significant impact on me is *Sabbath as Resistance: Saying No to the Culture of Now*. In a recent interview, I asked Brueggemann what he feels are the unique dangers of our globalized and technological world and how Sabbath provides a counternarrative or corrective. He answered, "The danger of globalized technology is to reduce everything and everyone to a commodity that can be used, administered, and given a price tag. Sabbath is an insistence that we and all others are neighbors, not commodities."[14] Sabbath works against propaganda and consumerism.

When I asked him to describe the underlying aim or goal of his extensive writing to the church, Brueggemann said:

> My continuing insistence in my work is that life is possible
> outside the domain of Pharaoh when it is lived according
> to the gospel of neighborly covenant. But that requires not
> simply personal resolve; it also requires a radically altered
> economic and political practice so that social relationships of
> another kind become normative.[15]

In other words, our competitive and consumerist framework is wholly insufficient for the kinds of relationships and societies Scripture points us to.

In that vein, I asked Brueggemann what charge he would give to next-generation leaders passionate about rethinking and reimagining the world through a theological lens. He answered, "Develop a well-informed critical capacity in order to see that what we regard as 'given' in our society is in fact a construct. When recognized as a construct, alternatives become imaginable and possible." In other words, we need to walk circumspectly, see multiple sides, and realize we have blind spots so that we can more passionately seek truth rather than defend ideology.

Words shape us. Society creates givens and norms. And, like the pro-war propaganda created under Woodrow Wilson in World War I, these norms then shape the thinking of generations.

The Voice from the Outside

One way of developing a critical capacity to see and evaluate what is a "given" in our society is to engage and listen to voices outside of it. I credit my friend Leroy for helping further open my eyes to the role of the "other" in Scripture and in God's plan to help us learn to see what we otherwise wouldn't see.

The "other" shows up numerous times in Scripture. It's there that Jesus uses the most unlikely of people, such as Samaritans, to instruct Jews about the kingdom of God. It's there when God uses the Ninevites to teach Jonah about forgiveness and the inclusive nature of His redemptive plan for the world. It's there when Jesus uses Mary Magdalene—unlikely from a gender perspective in His day and age—to teach the disciples the true nature of worship when she pours expensive perfume over Him. Jesus gives her, in some sense, primacy of place, saying, "Wherever the gospel is preached throughout the world, what she has done will also be told, in memory of her" (Mark 14:9).

The role of the other—the voice of the other as a teaching device in Scripture and in our lives—is vastly more significant than the credit we've ever given it. As Wendell Berry so aptly puts it, "It is not from ourselves that we learn to be better than we are."[16]

One of the more important facets of communication we learn in the modern world is that it is not just *what* someone says, but *who* says it. Content is not disconnected from the one sharing it. Life experience, age, race, gender, education, and more all converge to give nuance and color to the words we speak. Who are those people whose voice and presence can help us better understand what God has to say and how to walk in His will? Who is the "other" we are overlooking, the other who has been marginalized, the other who has been left behind? As Leroy likes to say, "We'll never truly know all of who God is unless we can connect to one another."[17]

Are they the old? The young? The poor? People from the inner city? Those living in the rich suburbs? Whoever we tend to look past or ignore as not being relevant may be the very ones God wants to speak to us through. Dorothy Day once said, "We must talk about poverty, because people insulated by their own comfort lose sight of it."[18]

Our conversations emerge from borrowed material. Maybe that's why God leans so heavily on the voice from the outside. A multiplicity of voices doesn't lead to propaganda. It isn't the advertising voice aimed to play on desire, and it isn't the echo chamber of our own culture reflecting back to us our own biases. Hearing a multiplicity of voices protects us from confirmation bias, like watering dry grass protects it from fire.

Maybe cross-cultural engagement, whether reading books, traveling, or simply finding conversation partners, could radically alter the words we use and how we use them. At the opening of the chapter, we quoted Jason Stanley's sage wisdom: "A society that is deeply affected by propaganda will be one in which certain legitimate routes that an individual's life path can take will be closed off."[19] May our communities be marked in deeper ways by robust conversation with a diversity of voices. May we open ourselves to hearing from God through all the channels He would use to teach us. May we identify the voice of propaganda for what it is: a siren song. And may we be free to pursue paths that lead us into the fullness of humanity God envisions for His children.

Chapter 3

The Challenge of Connecting in a Digital Age

We are drowning in information,
while starving for wisdom.

E. O. WILSON

The first time I (A. J.) can fully remember a trip to Disneyland, I was about nine. There were no cellphones back then. (Rather, there were no cellphones that did not require a nuclear-sized battery pack that could explode at a moment's notice.) For working people, going to Disneyland meant stepping out of the real world and into fantasy. Perhaps that's why I loved going to Disneyland with my dad so much. He was a successful doctor, but I knew that at Disneyland I would have him all to myself—without interruption.

I recently took my six-year-old son to Disneyland. One thing proved glaringly different from what I remembered. The rides were largely the same, the characters waited in the same place to have pictures taken, and the churros were as delicious—and as expensive—as ever. The difference was simple: smartphones.

As we stood in line after line, I looked down to find children pulling on their parents' shirts to get their attention. The parents were focused on their smartphones. While the negative effects of technology on children are slowly becoming more and more apparent,[1] I had never seen it as clearly with my own eyes as I did there. For the first time I began to see how these little devices were actually taking our hearts and minds to other places, away from the very ones we should love the most.

While we now have far more options and information, the digital age has drastically changed the nature of human relationships. It has increased our communication capacity, but it has decreased our attentiveness and ability to communicate well with the people in arms' reach. As evidenced by our growing reliance on phones and computers, it seems assumed as dogmatic truth that the digital age has brought us more happiness than ever before and infinitely improved our way of life. For many, however, this long unquestioned modern dogma is rightly beginning to be doubted.

In an *Atlantic* article published in 2017, author and consultant Jean M. Twenge, PhD, discusses whether smartphones have destroyed a generation, specifically post-millennials.[2] Generational differences have been the focus of Twenge's research for the last twenty-five years, beginning while she was a doctoral student in psychology. She points out that the characteristics that come to define a generation typically manifest themselves gradually. However, around 2012, she observed "abrupt shifts in teen behaviors and emotional states." Where the lines on her graphs had once been gentle slopes, they "became steep mountains and sheer cliffs, and many of the distinctive characteristics of the Millennial generation began to disappear."

Twenge had never seen anything like this in all her years analyzing generational data, especially among those born between 1995 and 2012—what Twenge calls the iGen generation. The only explanation she suggests for this radical shift in mental and relational health is that, in 2012, "the proportion of Americans who owned a smartphone surpassed 50 percent."

While generational changes have both positive and negative aspects, one of the most frightening issues iGenners face is a greater vulnerability to depression (and with it, suicide). Suicide rates have skyrocketed among this age group since 2011. And Twenge connects this directly to the digital explosion. "It is not an exaggeration," laments Twenge, "to describe iGen as being on the brink of the worst mental-health crisis in decades." She traces much of this personal deterioration to their phones. Teens from across the social spectrum are affected, regardless of race, ethnicity, economic status, or where in the country they live. Everyone's life has been altered by this digital awakening.

Few would question that there is always a litany of pressures that shape each generation of young people—war, technological leaps, parenting styles, cultural movements, scientific advances, or even a free concert on a muddy New York dairy farm. There is no single factor that ever defines a generation. While other factors contribute to generational change, Twenge asserts that it's the "twin rise of the smartphone and social media" that has caused "an earthquake of a magnitude we've not seen in a very long time, if ever."

Preferring Phones to Peers

These technological developments undoubtedly have dramatic effects—both good and negative—on human relationships. One concerning by-product has been the loss of conversation among younger individuals.

You may have noticed an odd trend in recent years, for example, of increased preference for text messaging over conversation, evidenced by a strange phenomenon we call *voice mail cramming*, whereby one fills their phone's voice mail with as many messages as it can hold so that the caller has to text. We don't want to talk; we just want the necessary information. Texting, in fact, provides just that—an opportunity for sanctified dialogue where we can write, edit, and re-edit before hitting the Send button. In short, it allows a space to not say anything that might be taken the wrong way—it keeps the real us from slipping out. Conversation does not allow such a medium. There is no editing. What is said is said and can't be taken back.

More than anything, texting and social media platforms give us the technological ability to multitask relationships. We can speak to a dozen people by text while also updating our social media accounts. These technologies provide a way for humans to have more and more relationships that operate at our convenience. We are multitasking one another, keeping each other safely in our inboxes and out of special reach.

A student in my church has experienced this head-on. She recently moved to Canada for a graduate program, but when she was living in Portland, she struggled to connect with people. Everyone seemed super busy all the time. They always texted but never had time for coffee. Yet after she left for Canada, all her Portland friends wanted to hang out and keep up a texting relationship. She reflected on this oddity, saying it seemed as though people were more interested in "having an acquaintance in Canada than having a deep friendship at home." She lamented that she felt used as a "texting buddy."

Often, texting can be a positive supplement to a healthy relationship with lots of face-to-face interaction, and this is to be celebrated. Certainly there *are* benefits to how connected our digital devices can keep us.

But sometimes we prefer text over talking because we do not have enough time for conversation and that relationship. Texting can become a survival mechanism to keep up with someone so you don't have to do the hard work of either entering the relationship or ending it. Texting is the lubricant that allows us to feel as though we're in constant contact while not forcing us to commit or actually give time to the relationship. And as our relationships become more and more thinly spread, one can only guess that our loneliness will increase proportionately with the number of texting and Snapchat friendships we maintain. The digital age pads our pride with a thin veneer of intimacy without forcing us to enter any of its sacred pain.

Because relationship and conversation are the messier and more difficult options, we increasingly choose the easier, less risky forms of communicating. For this and other reasons, iGenners demonstrate a preference for a relationship with their phone or iPads over relationships with peers. In 2015, only about 56 percent of high school seniors dated (compared to around 85 percent with boomers and Gen Xers). While this preference has resulted in some positive effects, such as the lowest teen birth rate—down

67 percent since 1991—the implications are insidious and far-reaching.[3]

Today's teens seem to be maturing much later. Unlike Gen X, who started becoming adults earlier and finished becoming adults later, today's eighteen-year-olds now act more like yesterday's fifteen-year-olds, and fifteen-year-olds behave more like thirteen-year-olds. Teens seem content to stretch childhood well into their high school years.

This is borne out in teens' reticence to take on the responsibilities that require engagement with the world. Twenge points out that fewer are working, and they delay obtaining drivers' licenses. They are content to spend more time at home in their rooms—but not because they love to study. Instead, they are on their phones, alone.

For all the time spent at home, teens' relationships with their parents are not any healthier than the generations that preceded them. Twenge relates the story of Athena, who is a self-professed expert at tuning out her parents. While Athena kept up with her friends over the summer, nearly all her contact with them was via text messages or over Snapchat. Athena said, "I've been on my phone more than I've been with actual people. My bed has, like, an imprint of my body." Athena typifies her generation. In fact, from 2000 to 2015, there was a 40 percent drop in the number of teens who got together daily with their friends.

We have more acquaintances, contacts, and text exchanges, yet we are unhappier than ever. While iGenners seem *content* to sequester themselves in their rooms and disengage from interacting with people, data suggest *they are not happy*. Twenge reports on a study that points out a glaring correlation:

Teens who spend more time than average on screen activities are more likely to be unhappy, and those who spend more time than average on nonscreen activities are more likely to be happy.

There's not a single exception.[4]

Unplugged

Not everyone has bought into the notion that the digital age is everything it promises to be. If spending time on their phones is actually making teens lonelier and far less happy, why do they do it?

In a 2012 *Psychology Today* article, Susan Weinschenk, PhD, examines the relationship between phones and dopamine. Dopamine was once believed to be the brain chemical that controls pleasure. With more research, scientists are reevaluating the effects of dopamine on behavior. They are finding that dopamine controls "seeking" behavior. That is, it causes us to want, desire, and seek. It makes us curious and directs goal-seeking behaviors. In fact, "the dopamine system is most powerfully stimulated when the information coming in is small so that it doesn't fully satisfy."[5] Short texts and 140-character tweets set dopamine levels raging. Is it any wonder that iGenners, whose brains were still developing as social media became ubiquitous, would rather spend time with their phones than with their friends?

Along these lines, former Facebook vice president for user growth Chamath Palihapitiya said in a recent interview that he feels "tremendous guilt" about the company he helped run. In an address at the Stanford Graduate School of Business, he told the audience, "I think we have created tools that are ripping apart the social fabric of how society works." Palihapitiya then recommended people take a "hard break" (like he has done) from social media.[6]

Palihapitiya did not limit his criticisms to Facebook. Rather, he speaks to the wider online ecosystem. "The short-term, dopamine-driven feedback loops we've created are destroying how society works." This type of interaction, he says, comes with "No civil discourse, no cooperation, misinformation, mistruth." He adds, "It's not an American problem.... This is a global problem."[7]

We are aware this chapter seems pretty damning with regard to social media, and it is not our intent to sound as though we are anti–social media—both of us have Facebook pages, Twitter accounts, and blogs. But, Twenge, Weinschenk, and Palihapitiya are naming what many of us already know deep inside: there are significant challenges and problems that come with our ever-increasing engagement with online media.

Whether or not you decide to take a "hard break" from social media, as Palihapitiya recommends, it is important to step back and try to gain a more objective view of a very subjective process. We need to evaluate our roles in the social media sphere. As Christians, we are called to speak life to a dying world. In order to do this, we need to carve out space where we can engage in real conversation.

In the words of Max Frisch, "Technology . . . [is] the knack of so arranging the world that we don't have to experience it."[8] It whisks us away from what is in front of us. And since social media and online engagement can so radically affect our relationships, it's important that we proactively think through its implications and make our choices accordingly, rather than simply being swept away in the riptide.

Creating Conversational Space

Evangelical forebear Carl Henry, long before this digital revolution, lamented what he envisioned coming:

> Twentieth-century technology has shaped a global village in which human beings are bombarded with more sights and sounds than in any previous generation in history. Words and events recovered from the ancient past, words and events of the pulsating present, words and events projected at tomorrow's frontiers clamor for attention and hearing. No generation since Babel has faced so massive a communications problem, and to none has belief in transcendent divine disclosures seemed more suspect, and the sense of divine authority less clear.[9]

Henry rightly saw the future. We *are* surrounded by a cacophony of words, sounds, and ideas, each knocking at the door of our attention, demanding to get our undivided care and compassion. All the while, they are making our relational network too broad. We don't seem to engage with the people in our spheres as we once did. The internet has enabled us to become "quivering masses of availability"—available to everyone, while we are currently unavailable to the ones in front of us.[10]

As a result, the demand for space free of the clamor is beginning to bubble to the surface in a new way. Take the rise in escape rooms, for example. Groups of two to six people pay twenty-five dollars per person to be together in a room for an hour, without phones or technological interruption. They are provided a mystery or problem to solve and collaborate to find the solution. Think of the murder-mystery parties that became so popular in the 1980s. One wonders if escape rooms have as much to do with a desire for solving mysteries as they do our deep human urge to actually be with people again.

This desire for human interaction is similarly evidenced in the "cuddle party" movement. Beginning around 2010, it became increasingly popular for consumers to pay by the hour for a person to cuddle with. Federal and local investigators looked into these arrangements, fearing they were fronts for prostitution. In fact, they were not. People were actually paying by the hour to simply cuddle with another human being. Does this not speak to a very deep human need? We are texting each other but not touching one another. The high-tech world has led to a low-touch experience, and our souls are withering because of it.

As digital living, which is abstract and disconnected, increasingly replaces relationships in which we are present with one another, we will continue to lose the backdrop of actual life as a context for conversation. Can we really be present with someone when we are secretly texting under the table? In tangible relationships, people are present and they listen to one another. Contrast this with modern "friendships," which have a phone serving to mediate contact.

One pastor described for us how youth would hesitate to open up in person, but would often divulge downloads of personal information via text. One student even asked, when questioned about a personal issue, if they could text it rather than say it.

If the vast majority of interpersonal contact (using the term loosely) is via text or tweet, then we have redefined or diminished aspects of what used to constitute a traditional relationship. The

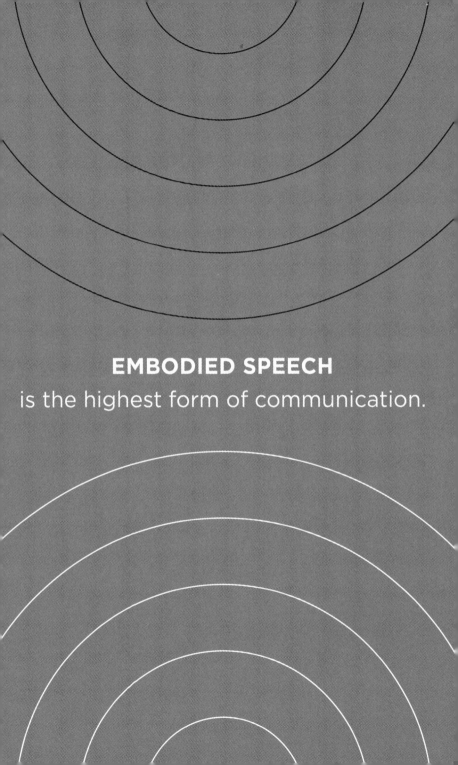

EMBODIED SPEECH
is the highest form of communication.

internet and social media have, in short, subverted the word *friend* and reduced relationship to something it was never meant to be.

Reloading God's Image

Living in a digital age is indeed challenging. The digital world serves us in many ways, but it fails us in many ways too. Because it is a world not likely to go away anytime soon, should we not learn how to converse in it in a Christlike, faithful way? We can start by centering ourselves on two key biblical themes.

First, we must recapture a theology of the incarnation. The digital life, with much of its communication absent of presence, can easily subvert the medium in which God speaks to humanity. The author of Hebrews writes, "In the past God spoke to our ancestors through the prophets at many times and in various ways, but in these last days he has spoken to us by his Son" (1:1–2). In both instances—that is, across God's long history of speaking—He used people. Flesh-and-blood people. God's communication was personal. Literally, incarnation means "becoming flesh."

Our digital mode of communication undermines this way of communicating. Texting, social media, email—these all depersonalize communication.

Are social media forms necessary parts of communicating in our world? Most likely. But we must learn to recapture the *incarnational* approach to communication God repeatedly modeled for us through the Old and New Testaments. Being "in the flesh" really does matter. Without it, we are left to offense and misunderstanding. Even more, we are deprived of sight, touch, sound, laughter. Binary code cannot replace physical friendship.

In pastoral work, one learns that people will forgive mean or errant words. People will forget texts and voice mails. But people do not forget who shows up. When someone is in the hospital, texts and messages come and go in someone's mind—but the person in the room with them is quietly written into their history forever. Incarnational or embodied speech is the highest form of communication. Words plus presence make a world of difference. People do not soon forget incarnational moments.

Second to reclaiming a theology of incarnation, we must re-capture a lived theology of the *imago Dei*—the image of God. The digital explosion has enabled us to forget the intrinsic worth and value of actual people who are made in the image of God. When you sit and read your Facebook feed or catch up on your texts or Twitter feed, all you see are little thumbnails of profile pictures. It is way easier to hate a thumbnail than a person. And the break-down of communication on social media is testimony to the fact that we less and less see others as created in the image of God, in-herently valuable in and of themselves.

Increasingly, we love people for their ideas or hate them for their ideas. In our world of freedom and mobility, we can easily create community with the people we love while ignoring and overlooking those we hate—all based on what they think. We no longer see and love people. We see and love ideas that fit our desires and wants, and we embrace the people who subscribe to them. In short, we often love ourselves more than others.

C. S. Lewis received many letters in his lifetime. So many that during the holidays he and his brother would spend up to eight hours a day responding. Even though C. S. Lewis was a professor and not a pastor, he believed it was his pastoral duty to respond to everyone in order to dignify and fulfill his responsibility to them. So voluminous was his correspondence that photocopies of his original letters fill a whole room of file cabinets at the Marion E. Wade Center at Wheaton College, and in the edited format by Walter Hooper, three massive volumes. A total of 3,274 of his letters have been preserved and an unknown number have been lost to history.[11]

Looking at the body of people with whom Lewis corresponded is amazing. He wrote to men and women of every stripe. He wrote to stay-at-home parents, people in prison, those leading churches, those sitting in pews, and even extensively to children. This practice more than anything revealed something of Lewis's theology. He didn't just write to the thought leaders or elite of his day. Rather, he wrote to the everyman and everywoman, because he believed that everyone is made in the image of God. All people, regardless of race, creed, or perceived cultural value, were worthy of his time, energy, concern, and a letter.

Our relationships begin to change once we fail to recognize and remember God's image in each and every person in this world. In fact, we must begin by remembering God's image in all people as a rationale for re-engaging relationship. I (Ken) recall a conversation with someone at a Christmas party a few years ago. He was examining the loss of civility in politics—why the political sphere seemed to be more fragmented than ever. His theory was that everything started to go downhill when air travel became normal. It used to be that we would elect our congresspersons to Washington, D.C., and they would live there all year long. A trip home would be rare for them. So, they would work, live, and eat together. As a result, the members of Congress would develop relationships across the aisle—with "the other side."

But then everything changed. Congresspersons were afforded the opportunity to fly home on the weekend. Today, it is actually common practice for congressmen and congresswomen to fly to their home districts on Thursday evening and return to Washington on Sunday evening. While it is good that they are in their districts spending time with their constituents, air travel has released them from having time to spend time with people of different viewpoints. They spend the bulk of their social time with constituents who elected them, and they do not socialize with those of another party. On this theory, some of the dysfunction in our political system is because Congresspersons ceased spending social time with their "enemies."

In the words of Martin Heidegger, "the frantic abolition of all distances brings no nearness."[12]

We used to be a people who would grab drinks with the "other side." Now, we do not even know them. Because we have increased mobility, getting away from the other is easier than ever. Before cars, planes, and buses, we were more obliged to love and engage those around us who were different.

This is why the blue states are getting *bluer* and the red states are getting *redder*. More often than not, our zip codes tell us how we vote—and we forget how to even speak respectfully of those with whom we disagree.

Nothing speaks more to what we believe about someone than *how* we communicate with them. And if we do not begin rightly with a strong understanding of the image of God in all people—as people of inherent dignity and worth—then we will never speak to them as such. When we forget the intrinsic worth of every person in the world, this is the result. We abandon the other. We leave them. Then we demonize them. This is the result of a culture that no longer sees the image of God in those "on the other side."

We must recapture that image, for without it we have no

reason to speak to those with whom we disagree. We need to begin to understand afresh how to communicate. In the end, our conversations are a piercing reflection of what we think of one another. Digital communication may reinforce our depersonalization of the other, but it doesn't have to.

Chapter 4

A Brief History of Information

The Kingdom of God is not in the wisdom of the world, nor in eloquence, but in the faith of the cross and in the virtue of dialogue.

ST. CYPRIAN

In the previous chapter, we explored the increasing challenges of communicating in a digital world, one marked by instantaneous and overwhelming connectivity and communication. But the framework for the digital world provides another challenge for communication—a world of information. This chapter explores the connection between our relationships and the information that we consume in a post-truth society.

From Cave Drawings to Bitcoin

Prior to the development of written languages, ideas were primarily communicated orally and visually. The ingenuity of our ancestors is fascinating.

Histories were once communicated through pictures drawn

or carved (as petroglyphs) on cave walls and rocks. In La Gomera of the Canary Islands, the inhabitants used a whistling language called Silbo Gomero to communicate with others across landscapes of deep valleys.[1] Beacon towers were located along the Great Wall of China so soldiers could use lights, fires, and smoke signals to communicate across great distances. Similarly, Indigenous Americans used smoke signals to warn of danger, provide news, or call people to gather. Smoke signals are actually believed to be one of the earliest forms of broadcast communication.

As for written texts, the Egyptians used tanned, stretched hides of goats, sheep, and cows to create papyrus and parchment. These media weighed a fraction of stone or clay tablets. This provided more space for information to travel faster and over longer periods of time. Prior to the fifteenth century, texts, pamphlets, and books had to be painstakingly copied by hand, or plates were hand-carved so the same text could be printed several times. This was still a time-consuming method for passing information to the masses. A general lack of literacy also limited who could read the information.

Everything changed in the 1440s when Johannes Gutenberg invented and slowly developed the first printing press. This revolutionized written information and perhaps marks the most important development in the spread of information until radio came along—similar to the invention of the internet. Gutenberg's press accelerated the process of printing copies of documents. While literacy rates were still very low, the Gutenberg press made texts more readily available and cheaper. This had a dramatic effect on literacy rates in Europe going forward. This newly invented means of spreading information was followed up by the Industrial Revolution in the eighteenth century, which brought about an unprecedented era of production, consumption, and consumerist patterns in human culture—particularly in the West.

Gutenberg helped usher in the Industrial Revolution, which ultimately led to the digital age, which roughly began in the 1960s.[2] The advent of the computer and the proliferation of digital information have brought about changes at an ever-increasing rate. The age of information is marked by the storage, compression, and immediate publication of all kinds of information through globalized and interconnected systems and structures.[3] In this age, argues author and historian James Gleick, "What's not going to pass is the centrality of information in all of our lives."[4] No longer is access to information limited by *where* one resides. Information is readily available to any and all—at least to any and all who have a computer or a smartphone.

We don't need to know the complete history of information dissemination to know how unhindered access to information is different from the way things once were. A single glance at this chart gives the picture.

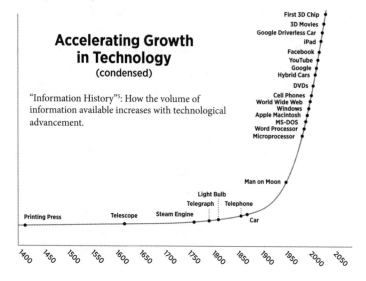

Accelerating Growth in Technology (condensed)

"Information History"[5]: How the volume of information available increases with technological advancement.

Media Psychology and
Magnetic Resonance Imaging

How we receive information changes the way we relate to information itself.

Looking especially at history since the invention of the Gutenberg press some six hundred years ago, we can see the speeding up of our world. Particularly in this information age, we have seen the ready availability of not only books, radio, and television but also computers. They have become more affordable and can process greater volumes of data with ever-increasing speed. We have seen the pervading influence of social media, computers, telephones, television and movies, and the internet. In most places, there is no escaping one or more of these things outside of moving beyond the reach of cell towers and Wi-Fi.

There are good and bad aspects associated with such constant access. For example, some educators effectively use computers and virtual reality (VR) to teach. Imagine "seeing" the art of the Louvre using VR. Things that might otherwise have been out of reach are now available for many people. That said, some people retreat to media technology to avoid the real life around them. For them, it becomes a mental and emotional refuge.

Media is such a centerpiece in our lives that media psychology is now a subspecialty within psychology, exploring the effects of the information age on the human mind. According to Dr. Bernard Luskin, Magnetic Resonance Imaging (MRI) is yielding fascinating research, and the results are providing some very specific insights on the brain and behavior.[6] In recent years, scientists have been able to validate the reality of what they call Internet Addiction Disorder or IAD. What they have found among those addicted to the internet and information consumption are types of withdrawal symptoms typically associated with substance addiction: tremors, shivers, nausea, and anxiety.[7] Scientists have classified IAD with other pathological behaviors such as gambling and eating disorders.

THE GOOD MEDIA EFFECTS:

- ▶ IQs are rising, according to the Education Testing Service. Much of the increase is due to advances in media assisted learning and interactive game playing.
- ▶ Girls are advancing in the field of science. Some studies attribute this to increased numbers of females engaging in interactive game play.
- ▶ The nexus between media and learning is increasingly popular and we are learning more about learning.
- ▶ Communication is increasing across cultures.
- ▶ Media has helped foster public understanding of many crucial issues.

THE BAD MEDIA EFFECTS:

- ▶ Attention spans are decreasing because of exposure to excessively stimulating and fast-paced media. A direct link between exposure to media stimulation and Attention Deficit Disorder (ADD) has surfaced from research.

- Violence in media causes desensitization to violence. It may facilitate violent acts. Violence may be contagious by observational learning and social agreement.
- Media-assisted crimes like identity theft and child pornography are taking new forms.
- Average number of sleep hours per night decreases in inverse proportion to the average number of hours per day of Internet use.
- Internet Addiction Disorder (IAD) is increasingly diagnosed by professional.[8]

We should be cautious. Like so many things, media is not inherently bad. What can be detrimental is *how* these forms of media are used and the *extent* to which they are used. The same technology that can be used to incite a revolution against a dictatorship can be used to make child pornography available to the general public. Technology is not good or bad; it's used for good or bad.

Too Much Information

The proliferation of information in our culture has led to a number of negative developments. First, it has led to information overload. In his book *The Organized Mind*, *New York Times* bestselling author Daniel J. Levitin describes a study that simulated a military exercise.[9] In the study, university students were told they could control the amount of information they received. In truth, they couldn't, but they were unaware of this. Their responses were used to study optimum levels of information. During the thirty-minute game period, student players were given either two, five, eight, ten, twelve, fifteen, or twenty-five pieces of information.

The theory of optimal information posited that the players would function better with approximately ten to twelve pieces of information. The experiment confirmed this number. The study's findings suggest that there are finite limits for the amount of information consumers can absorb and process in a given period of time. Levitin explains that it has been empirically demonstrated that more information leads to poorer choices by consumers. In a home-buying situation, you might be looking at two different houses, but you don't want to keep track of more than ten pieces of information about the two houses combined. Alternatively, you could choose to look at two parameters—like neighborhood and square footage—and then expand the number of houses for comparison to five. More than this is information overload. And multitasking is just another name for trying to juggle too much information.

We can consume information at whatever rate we desire. And we consume a ton of information. It has been said that just one hundred years ago, the average person would encounter as much information in a lifetime as is found in a daily *New York Times* newspaper today.

For many of us, despite all the information and venues to communicate available, we experience less joy, peace, and happiness than ever. It's as if we're shoving food into our mouths faster than we can chew and savor it. Even the best cuisine loses all its value if we don't have the time to enjoy it. What is the mind to do with all the piles of information acquired, each requiring attention and demanding a response? Can we actually be reflective and respond faithfully when we are drowning in information?

Second, the proliferation of information has led to an increase in information as entertainment—what one might call *infotainment*. Because we encounter so much information, the human mind has less and less attention to give. "When information is cheap" writes James Gleick, "attention becomes expensive."[10] And since the average person has less and less attention to give, those who are seeking to get our attention have turned to making information even more tantalizing.

The constant bombardment of information eventually numbs us, which leads to a third problem: sensationalism. When we are overloaded, only the sensational grabs our attention. Eventually, we crave it more and more. As a result, we change *where* we get our information. We used to look to teachers, news outlets, pastors, and others as authority figures to pass along both key information as well as the necessary frameworks for evaluating it. The old way had a neat hierarchical pyramid of information transmission and evaluation. The pyramid crumbles as information hits us from all directions. We instead curate our own information, choosing from a vast list of both traditional and nontraditional sources and figures we regard as trustworthy or authoritative.

One by-product of this privatized way of taking in information is that it isolates us from one another—even from our most important attachments. For example, when students go off to college and begin to understand their world in a different way, it often creates a chasm with their parents. When they come home for Christmas or Thanksgiving, they don't know how to talk to their parents about what they are learning. In many cases, the information they are taking in runs counter to that which their parents gave them long ago. And because they almost never see one another anymore, they don't have surplus time to talk. So, to save face and make Thanksgiving and Christmas as nice as possible, they don't actually talk about what they are learning.

This leads to, among other things, a kind of latent distrust and cynicism. Parents not trusting children or education. Children dismissing the teachings of elders or tradition. Students becoming more confrontational and not trusting the teachings of their professors. And our minds become museums of opinions, each artifact guarded by a rope and a plaque that reads "Do not touch. For observing only."

Another glaring problem with this deluge of information is that, as we begin to curate it ourselves, we can be choosy about what we collect and what we do not. There is a marketplace of ideas from which we can pick. No longer do we have to take in the information that has been given to us; instead, we can proactively seek out the information we *want* in order to support our biases and preconceived ideas. This has led to what has been called our post-truth era, where truth can be whatever we want it to be.

An egregious example of our post-truth reality is Holocaust denial. There are people who flat-out deny that six million Jews were systematically killed by the German war machine. Deborah E. Lipstadt is an American professor of Holocaust studies and the author of *Denying the Holocaust, History on Trial*, and *The Eichmann Trial*.[11] The book *History on Trial* tells the story of the *Irving v. Penguin Books Ltd.* case, which was filed in an English court by British author David Irving. Irving is the author of several books about the German leaders of World War II, which paint Hitler in a more favorable light. Lipstadt's *Denying the Holocaust* asserted that Irving had deliberately distorted evidence in his assertions about the Holocaust in order to match them with his ideological viewpoints.

In reaction to Lipstadt's books, Irving filed a libel suit against Lipstadt and her publisher. Since English libel law places the burden of proof on the defense, it was up to the attorneys for

Lipstadt and her publisher to defend her claims. Lipstadt won her case in 2000.

In an April 2017 TEDx talk, Deborah Lipstadt shared her reaction to first hearing about Holocaust deniers:

> The first time I heard about Holocaust denial, I laughed. . . . For deniers to be right, who would have to be wrong? . . . The bystanders. . . . The Poles [in Poland], who lived in towns and villages around the death camps, who watched day after day as the trains went in . . . and came out empty.[12]

She adds that the perpetrators themselves would have to be wrong too—"The people who say, 'We did it. I did it.' . . . In not one war crimes trial since the end of World War II has a perpetrator of any nationality ever said, 'It didn't happen.'"[13]

Clearly, there is an insurmountable burden of proof to overcome with regard to the Holocaust. Yet because "truth" has stopped being an absolute or tied to historical reality, people are choosing their truths and being willing to believe, embrace, and propagate a lie.

Delusional is the word many of us might use to describe someone who claims the Holocaust never happened—or that any other empirically provable event is a lie. Sadly, we see more and more of this happening; the post-truth era has brought us the Flat Earth Society as well.

Returning to Relating

Ralph Keyes, author of *The Post-Truth Era*, explains that we once had distinct boundaries between truth and lies. While we may still have what we call truth and lies, we also have "statements that may not be true but we consider too benign to call false."[14] We employ euphemisms. *Spin* has replaced *deceive*. We don't accuse people of lying but of "misspeaking" or being "economical with the truth." Keyes goes on:

> This is post-truth. In the post-truth era, borders blur between truth and lies, honesty and dishonesty, fiction and nonfiction. . . . Research suggests that the average American tells lies on a daily basis. These fibs run the gamut from "I like sushi," to "I love you."[15]

Casual dishonesty has led Human Resources departments to assume most résumés are padded. We see embellished lives on social media sites. We are dubious of the things we see and read there.

Blurring the lines between truth and lies yields ethical or moral relativism. What lays between truth and lies—right and wrong—is indeed a shaky foundation on which to build a society or relationships. As a result of a truth that is one thing for you and another for me, we enter relationships wary and skeptical, perhaps even afraid. How can we possibly enter authentic conversation if the truth is a constantly moving target and we feel we must question everything?

When objectivity is gone and we are willing to negotiate the sanctity of words, we are in trouble. In *Studies in Words*, C. S. Lewis uses a very interesting word, *verbicide*, to talk about the death or murder of a word or concept through improper use. Lewis writes:

The greatest cause of verbicide is the fact that most people are obviously far more anxious to express their approval and disapproval of things than to describe them. Hence the tendency of words to become less descriptive and more evaluative; then to become evaluative, while still retaining some hint of the sort of goodness or badness implied; and to end up by being purely evaluative.[16]

For Lewis, evaluative speech murders meaning. Words become corpses that we dress up to mean whatever we want them to. They either speak to true things and point us toward goodness, or they become merely evaluative, tools we use to point people not to the good, true, or beautiful, but in the direction of our opinion of the day.

Verbicide and post-truth go hand in hand. Enough people speaking the same lies over and over can establish an alternate reality that's every bit as powerful as what's actually true. George Bernard Shaw is right: "Syllables govern the world."[17] If we bend words to our opinions, then there is no longer any truth.

We do not have agreed-upon ethics about what words mean and how they are to be used. The internet allows us to create hashtags, bend phrases, and craft words for effect more than meaning. In some ways, promotion often wins out over pertinence. We have become language colonizers—forcing words to mean to us what we want them to be, rather than respect them for what they are and what they represent. We make words and language serve our own purposes. And in a post-truth age where we can essentially get away with bending reality to our words rather than the other way around, we have become ethical relativists more than we would want to admit. We're all deniers at some level. We may not deny the Holocaust, but do we kill truth to our advantage, reshaping narratives to our liking?

As Lipstadt asserted in her TEDx talk, "Deniers are wolves in sheep's clothing." She continues emphatically and conclusively, "There are facts and there are opinions. . . . And there are lies."[18]

Chapter 5

Here Be Dragons

Language is a way of negotiating relationships.

STEVEN PINKER

More than two thousand years ago, the Roman philosopher Seneca stated, "We are more often frightened than hurt; and we suffer more from imagination than from reality."[1] We have all probably experienced this at some point in our lives. This seems to be endemic to humankind. Seneca understood this. Perhaps he was looking at the maps of his time.

A long time ago only a portion of the world had been explored and mapped by Western Europeans. The areas beyond the known world, understandably, had to be identified in some fashion. The ancient Roman cartographers began to indicate such places with the inscription *hic svnt leones* (i.e., "Here be lions"). They weren't alone in letting their imaginations wander. This practice continued into medieval times. During the Middle Ages, cartographers began indicating the unknown in an even more imaginative way, one which clearly indicated a particular fear. They began using the image of dragons, sea serpents, and other dangerous creatures. This hinted at the harm sailors imagined encountering as they entered previously uncharted waters.

For example, on the Anglo-Saxon *Mappa Mundi* (world map) that was created in England around 1025, the picture of a dragon appears in the upper left-hand corner. The British Isles are depicted in the map's lower left, and east is at the top of the map. In this way, the cartographer was indicating that lands to the east were unexplored.

While we use the phrase about dragons as a popular means for referring to such maps, this phrase never actually appears in English on any map. In fact, the only documented use of this phrase on a map is in Latin—*hc svnt dracones* ("Here be dragons"), appearing on the Hunt-Lenox Globe (circa 1510). This small globe is the earliest such engraving, dating to the period immediately following the discovery of the New World.

While the maps of our era that depict dragons appear mainly on fantasy and role-playing games now, the phrase *Here be dragons* has evolved to mean something entirely different. For example, computer programmers use it to denote code that is unintelligible but nevertheless works. The phrase now serves as a warning to other programmers to not tweak the code for fear of breaking it.

Like medieval explorers and modern-day programmers, we won't venture conversationally to certain places for fear of what we might encounter.

Mature Conversations

During the civil rights movement, Martin Luther King Jr. said, "In the end, we will remember not the words of our enemies but the silence of our friends." His observation was specific to the difficult conversations on race in the America of his day, but it speaks to a larger tendency of avoiding truth because of fear. King was speaking about our reticence to go where things feel unsafe.

For much of the last twenty years, I (Ken) have been studying and speaking on biblical and social justice. One of my primary purposes for this focus was to challenge the evangelical church to see and reprioritize social justice in its thinking and programming. Often, however, I find Christian leaders or laypersons who have a very strong reaction to the phrase *social justice*.

Their responses almost invariably take the form, "Social justice is a slippery slope toward falling victim to the social gospel." Slippery-slope arguments are a standard logical fallacy in any college book on logic, but fear can often make us steer clear even when truth would have us walk closer.

However, most can't tell me one thing about the social gospel movement, neither its strengths nor its weaknesses. For the most part, it is just code language that not only leverages fear but also provides justification for remaining silent and aloof.

It seems so strange that something about which the Bible speaks so often—justice—could become a suspect word to the people who are called out and ordered by the God of love and justice.

The history of religious movements and politics in the States has made some conversations off-limits among more conservative Christian circles and society.[3] In this instance, dragons—which once designated the margins of knowledge—keep us from the margins of society.

How do we combat this fear? We have hard conversations.

From the 1930s to 1940s, C. S. Lewis met with a group of literary friends on Tuesdays to share beer and read one another's unfinished works at a pub in Oxford. They called themselves the Inklings. The Inklings included J. R. R. Tolkien, Charles Williams, and Lewis's brother, Warren. Of the Inklings, Warren wrote, "We were no mutual admiration society. . . . To read to the Inklings was a formidable ordeal."[4]

Forged in this crucible of criticism were C. S. Lewis's *The Screwtape Letters* and Narnia series and Tolkien's *The Hobbit*. Had it not been for Lewis's challenges, Tolkien said he'd never have published *The Lord of the Rings*.

Like the Inklings, a Christian church isn't an admiration society. We are transformed not through flattery but by doing what is best for one another. Perhaps this is why Henry Ward Beecher famously said, "Every man should keep a fair-sized cemetery in which to bury the faults of his friends."

Hard conversations are one of the forgotten arts of healthy Christian living. Trends indicate we shuttle ourselves out of these kinds of conversations with great regularity. In *The Big Sort*, Bill Bishop examines how the American social scene has largely sorted itself out by homogeneous, like-minded people for the last thirty years.[5] The danger in this is that we not only believe more strongly in our previously held beliefs, but we increasingly marginalize those who hold divergent beliefs. Psychologists have long observed this effect.

I (Ken) recently met with an African American friend named Adam, who is finishing a doctoral dissertation on religious forms in the transatlantic slave trade. His specific concentration is on religious practices and Christian engagement during the Middle Passage, the horrific middle leg of the slave triangle, wherein Africans were tightly packed in slave ships and shipped to the Americas.

Over brunch, we discussed the Justice Conference Adam had attended in Cape Town, South Africa. He was very impressed by the quality of the speakers, as well as the forthright engagement

To reflect on how our society has advantaged some while disadvantaging others—and address the spiritual implications of our responsibility for our neighbor—is to agree with God that **WE *ARE* OUR BROTHER'S KEEPER.**

with the extremely difficult and seemingly intractable issues of race, land, and injustice—issues being openly addressed in a country with a complicated colonial history. The Christian speakers spoke candidly. Rather than shying away from such a hot-button issue, they found it necessary to talk about the imperative role of Christians in restorative justice and reconciliation.

We are only able to enter into such honest and difficult conversations when space is created to first name, and then deconstruct, any given topic and its effects on theology, the life of the church, and the world. There is tremendous power in opening up relationship to difficult conversations about important things. Such discomfort has transformative and generative power.

Simultaneously, there is great harm done when we do not talk about issues that are at the core. I (Ken) was talking with the chaplain of a Christian college recently. He had reached out to me because he felt convicted about white privilege and the continued prevalence of racism in America, and he wanted advice on what he should do.

We talked about the need to listen, lament, and learn (from people outside his comfort zone), to be willing to lay down or steward his privilege, and to not shy away from uncomfortable conversations. Toward the end of the conversation, he asked me to later speak at the college's chapel service. I said that a chapel service might be a great time to bring in a multicultural panel to help us lean into this conversation with students, especially on some of the deeper nuances of race and privilege. His reply shocked me. "We can't do that," he said. "The higher ups specifically forbade me from ever having the words *white privilege* mentioned from our chapel stage."

To reject discussions about privilege is to agree with Cain, who asked sarcastically, "Am I my brother's keeper?" To welcome such a conversation—to reflect on how our society has advantaged some while disadvantaging others and address the spiritual implications of our responsibility for our neighbor—is to agree with God that we *are* our brother's keeper.

This is not to disparage anyone. Rather, it is to serve in the process of opening ourselves up to honest self-reflection, where we can sit with the tension of conversation. A critical step to redeeming how we talk is opening ourselves up to these redemptively difficult conversations. If we can't have these conversations from the podium at a Christian college, then what are we saying about our pursuit of truth and justice? If not at academic Christian institutions, then *where* should we look for mature Christian conversations? Should we have maps with "Here be dragons" written in the margins? Or should we live confidently in faith that exploration and mature conversations are where discoveries can be made, where iron sharpens iron?

For the most part, the role of the biblical prophets was always to bring a strong and disruptive voice *to their own* communities. If they were preaching to another community, we'd call them missionaries or emissaries from God. We still have prophets because we still need course correction and fresh eyes on our historic reality.

Contrary to the view that addressing race, colonialism, or privilege divides the church, holding a biblical mirror to American Christianity is neither unloving nor divisive. The church *needs*— as it always has—the presence of prophetic voices challenging the status quo and bringing reformation.

Difficult conversation composed of well-chosen words and space to consider new thoughts is a way we can pursue wisdom and challenge ourselves to more fully walk in the ways of Jesus.

All Things to All People, or the Law of Love

In a world where travel has become commonplace and where the church is more visible to a watching world, it becomes incredibly important for us to think through the implications of global conversational ethics and the role of respect and empathy in the love of neighbor.

As Paul, a missionary and world traveler in his own right, said:

Though I am free and belong to no one, I have made myself a slave to everyone, to win as many as possible. To the Jews I became like a Jew, to win the Jews. To those under the law I became like one under the law (though I myself am not under the law), so as to win those under the law. To those not having the law I became like one not having the law (though I am not free from God's law but am under Christ's law), so as to win those not having the law. To the weak I became weak, to win the weak. I have become all things to all people so that by all possible means I might save some. I do all this for the sake of the gospel, that I may share in its blessings. (1 Cor. 9:19–23)

"I have become all things," Paul said. In a world of division, where we regularly point out the differences of others, Paul sought to step into the experience of the other.

We see this in the way Paul preached. In the three Pauline sermons recorded in Acts, we discover something quite unique about his method. In Antioch of Pisidia, he preached in a Jewish synagogue both to Jews and to Gentiles who were known as "God-fearers" (Acts 13:16–41). There, Paul *begins* his sermon with extensive Jewish history and a reflection on the Old Testament narrative. In a sermon in Athens, Paul *begins* his sermon to the Areopagus—those who live in the center of Greek philosophy and poetic creativity—with a conversation about local religious worship by quoting the Greek poets (Acts 17:22–31). Finally, in Lystra, Paul preaches to what William Barclay called the "wilds"—superstitious rural bumpkins who would have known next to nothing of Jewish history, Old Testament law, or Greek philosophy (Acts 14:15–17).[6] In the rural world, Paul *begins* his sermon with words about nature—the sun, the wind, the rain, and things that grow from the ground.

Barclay describes Paul's conversational brilliance:

> He had the gift of beginning where his hearers were. . . .
>
> The significant fact is that in the three sermons the approach, at least on the surface, is completely different. . . . In his missionary approach Paul had no set scheme and formula; his approach was completely flexible. *He began where his audience was.*[7] [emphasis added]

Conversation requires us to follow the model of Jesus—as Paul did—by stepping into the shoes of the other in order to love and serve them. Thinking through how our words affect others is a transformative step in equipping the church to better live its mission of being salt and light.

Rarely do we have serious discussions about cross-cultural interactions outside of classes in colleges or universities. But because we live in a world where we're speaking across borders daily through social media and travel, then Paul's words must be a guide for our engagement with others.

One of the darkest chapters in American Christianity was our American Indian missionary activity. Christians in early America—the vast majority of whom were not ethnic Jews—had become believers without having to first convert to Judaism. These believers, however, took a hypercritical and destructive approach to American Indians. They believed the native culture was somehow corrupt or uncivilized from a Christian perspective and that American Indians, therefore, needed to both convert to Jesus *and* adopt the ways of Western Christian civilization.

The long, horrible history was one that included forced schooling where dress, language, hair, and even names had to conform to Anglo-Saxon Christian ideals. *Soap* was the first English word that many young American Indians learned well because it was used to wash out their mouths when they started speaking in their native tongue or refused to go by their newly given Christian names. The phrase that became attached to this era of forced conversion was "Kill the Indian in him, and save the man."[8] In civilizing the native, the ends justified the means. That is, it was perfectly acceptable to obliterate his or her identity, heritage, and culture as long as you were doing a service to his or her soul.

As Gentiles, we didn't feel pressure to convert to Judaism—adopting their diet, traditions, and ceremonies—in order to be saved in a similar "Kill the Gentile, save the man" approach. Yet we felt compelled to do exactly this to American Indians on a massive scale. We reversed Paul's argument in the book of Galatians and became like the Judaizers, only this time as Western Christianizers. People had to appropriate whiteness and Western culture to be considered civilized, respectable, and—ultimately—Christian.

A friend once illustrated this hypocrisy by saying that a devil-worshiping heavy metal drummer could get saved and a month later be playing drums in the worship band of a suburban church without anyone saying anything, but when American Indians from the reservation became Christians in his childhood church, they were told they could never pick up their drums again because they were relics from a heathen culture.

Without empathy, which requires identification with the other, it is truly impossible to understand the other. If we are not willing to see from the vantage point of the person we seek to love, we cannot call it love.

Empathy and identification, however, only work when sets of language that would apply to me also apply to the other. When we employ words like "merciless Indian savages"—a phrase appearing in America's Declaration of Independence—it undercuts our empathy. Or when we look at an inhabited land and appropriate Old Testament imagery around the Promised Land into a colonial theology—underscoring the idea of manifest destiny (that God gave white Western Christian culture this land from "sea to shining sea"), it erodes empathy. If Indians are savages, and if they are typecast like the Philistines or the Canaanites of old, then it is not hard to see how people saw themselves as a Joshua, Gideon, or King David. God was at their backs, while these people—the "others"—stood in a place where they could be erased, removed, or converted.

What happened to the Christian mission of grafting people of every tribe, tongue, and nation into the one head, Jesus Christ? Contrast this with missionaries such as Hudson Taylor who dressed like, lived with, and spoke in the language of his *adopted* culture. The gospel doesn't require that we shed all the background of our culture and heritage. Instead, it means that, within our culture and heritage, we seek to know and glorify God in the name of Christ by living as people who are redeemed and called to transcend the differences that once kept us at odds with one another.

Imagine a missionary to a foreign land who refuses to learn the tongue of the tribe he is serving. How practical would it be if he goes and expects all the native individuals to learn *his* language? This is unfathomable. Learning another's language is, perhaps, the most missional and Christlike activity one can take up. If we want to reach someone with the love of Christ, we must first step into *their* world on *their* terms.

Yet, in relationship and conversation, we often demand everyone else shift their focus and attention to meet our expectations and needs. To be healthy communicators, we must choose willingly and humbly to bear the cross of stepping into another's world—not the other way around. When we learn another's story, convictions, background, and experience, we are more apt at understanding that person and knowing how best to speak to him or her. And, more importantly, we're able to see how much common ground we really have. This only comes through listening.

Yes, and . . .

How can we make a difference in the way we talk about difficult things with others? One of the more interesting books on this topic is the book *Yes, And*, by Kelly Leonard and Tom Yorton. Leonard and Yorton are executives at The Second City in Chicago, the improv theater that gave us Bill Murray, Steve Carell, and Tina Fey, to name just a few from its long list of alumni.

As the title suggests, the book focuses on the phrase "Yes, and . . . ," which is the first rule of improv. In good improv, you not only affirm what another scene-mate initiates ("yes"), but you add to it ("and . . ."). This affirmational and generative "yes, and . . ." discipline not only leads to great comedy; it can lead to great living. Years of experience have demonstrated that these two small words reap huge benefits.

Many of us find "No" an all-too-easy response to a question. One of the quickest ways to shut a person down, make him or her feel defensive, or kill communication is to simply say no. The word *no* ends a conversation. "No" cuts off opportunity and creativity and leaves only the binary option of acquiescence or argument.

Conversely, "Yes, and . . ." invites collaboration, cooperation, and creativity. It fosters relationship. To offer the words "Yes, and . . . ," we must be present in the moment and actively listening. As Leonard and Yorton explain, "Deep, practiced listening is really a form of meditation. It is a skill that enables you to turn off the judgment part of your brain and allows you to interact with individuals and groups in a seamless way."[9]

Answering in the affirmative and authentically offering your own contribution allows every idea to be validated and for participants to be struck by both surprise and innovation. "Yes, and . . ." is motivating and encourages cocreation. The authors point out that "none of us is as smart as all of us."[10]

In the same way that explorers could only chart waters by venturing into them, so we can only chart knowledge and relationship by venturing in—and we do that through "Yes, and . . ." World-famous improvisers T. J. Jagodowski and Dave Pasquesi did this countless times in their two-man show, *TJ & Dave*. They began each show by walking onstage in the dark. After several seconds, the lights would come up and they'd survey the audience. Then they'd survey each other. All of this was slow, uncalculated, and quiet. And then with no fanfare, no strategy, no plan, they'd begin, simply responding to the minuscule impressions they got from the audience and from each other. An hour later, audiences would leave amazed that the two men created whole worlds before their eyes—all from simply looking around.

Fear cuts off communication. Confidence breeds it.

As we follow Christ, it would do us good to remember that He said, "I am the way and the *truth* and the life" (John 14:6). Through this we can shed the fear of the unpredictability of conversation and find the confidence to go to the edges of maps, knowing that the Spirit of truth will guide us.

We live in a world in which we're all waiting to be heard. That seems to be the mantra of our time, doesn't it? Less and less are we having conversation with others. We are replacing real conversation with simply waiting for others to finish what they are saying so we can get in what we have to say. Conversations have largely ceased to be places where we actually engage with other people's words. Most of us long to be better listeners, better conversationalists, and better friends. But we often slip back into patterns of disengagement or overspeaking.

It is interesting that comedy and improv can demonstrate a skill that should be a habitual part of business, friendship, and family conversational habits. "Yes, and . . ." also teaches us something about our speech as Christians. In Ephesians 4:29, Paul confidently exhorts us to "not let any unwholesome talk come out of [our] mouths, but only what is helpful for building others up according to their needs, that it may benefit those who listen." "No" might not be unwholesome, but rarely is it contributive or edifying. "Yes, and . . ." offers the gift of validation, of building—the gift of real relationship.

There is something about the Spirit of God that is likened to the furthering of possibilities and individuals. He has told us that with Him all is possible. "For no matter how many promises God has made, they are '*Yes*' in Christ. And so through him the '*Amen*' is spoken by us to the glory of God" (2 Cor. 1:20).

The apostle Paul became all things to all people, choosing to speak their language and to discuss the nature of God on *their* terms, not his own. He wandered outside of the map that Jewish culture drew and into communities he learned to understand and appreciate, even while testifying to them about Jesus.

In his work *Life Together*, Bonhoeffer says, "The Christian, too, belongs not in the seclusion of a cloistered life but in the thick of foes. There is his commission, his work."[11] He then quotes Luther:

> The Kingdom is to be in the midst of your enemies. And he who will not suffer this does not want to be of the Kingdom of Christ; he wants to be among friends, to sit among roses and lilies, not with the bad people but the devout people. . . . If Christ had done what you are doing who would ever have been spared?[12]

If Christ had done what you are doing, who would ever have been spared? I'm not sure Jesus would be proud of us when religious purity becomes the excuse for failing to draw near to the margins.

Here be dragons began as a warning, but to Paul, the world's first missionary, it would have seemed more like an invitation. May we, too, accept the invitation to live and learn in the margins of our maps and so fulfill the law of love.

Part 2

THE WORDS OF GOD

Accurate speech about anything, and especially about God, is in fact a rhythm of silence and speech, speaking and listening.

ELLEN DAVIS,
Getting Involved with God

Chapter 6

Jesus Speaks

It is not easy to convey a sense of wonder, let alone resurrection wonder, to another. It's the very nature of wonder to catch us off guard, to circumvent expectations and assumptions. Wonder can't be packaged, and it can't be worked up. It requires some sense of being there.

EUGENE H. PETERSON

As soon as all the people saw Jesus, they were overwhelmed with wonder and ran to greet him.

MARK 9:15

On Mondays I (A. J.) go quiet. There is a Catholic monastery down the road called the Grotto where several nuns and priests live. There is also a beautiful church there. On Mondays I turn off my phone, leave my computer, bring my Bible, and sit in the quiet. I'm not the only one—other worshipers come to find respite from the noise of Portland to contemplate God and His goodness.

But the Grotto is also a well-known tourist attraction. It's not uncommon to sit in the space and see people come in to take pictures. It can be a little awkward, the dance between those who have come into the beautiful, sacred space to go inward and find God in silence, and those who come to take pictures, shuffling their feet and clicking their cameras.

For some, beauty is a gift that assists us to go inward, to seek the deep things of God. For others, it is more something to be commodified or captured.

Life is, indeed, full of "you had to be there" moments. And of course, there's nothing wrong with trying to capture them with a photo. Many of our richest and most beautiful experiences—a majestic sun melting over the Pacific, a radiant bride walking down the aisle, a child's brave performance in his first school play—leave even the most skilled and eloquent speaker at a loss for words when trying to describe them. And sharing those experiences can be good. This explains why it is estimated that more than 1.3 trillion photos will be taken across the globe this year. As much as we hate to use the weary cliché, we instinctively know that a picture really is worth a thousand words. This is why we draw on whiteboards during meetings and use PowerPoint presentations. If we utilize artistic media to communicate, illustrate, or underscore what we are saying, it should be no surprise that God does the same.

To be sure, humans have always been drawn to images. We inherently understand visual metaphors because we learned to attach meaning to images at an early age, long before we could describe what we were seeing with words. Within a few weeks of arriving in the world, a baby begins to associate visual stimuli with significance. A glimpse of its mother is quickly translated into, "I'm about to be fed" or "I'm not alone." Images have a way of instantly communicating those things that could never be said with words.

The first mention of "image" in the Bible is in the creation account, when God creates humans in His image and likeness (Gen. 1:27). Humans are uniquely formed to be God's physical representation in His world. We aren't God, but we bear His likeness, such that when we see another human being, we are getting a glimpse of our Creator. The word *image* appears five times in the book of Genesis and always in reference to the image of God stamped upon humanity. It doesn't show up again until we read about the Ten Commandments in Exodus 20. The ritual or symbolic forms of religion that God has ordained for all seem to be aimed at artistically underscoring the reality of the first of the Ten Commandments—"You shall have no other gods before me" (v. 3).

The Pulitzer Prize–winning poet Archibald MacLeish once wrote, "Anything can make us look, only art can make us see."[1] *Looking* is entering the Grotto and snapping a photo. *Seeing* is entering and meeting God.

The Incarnation

"In the beginning was the Word, and. . . . The Word became flesh" (John 1:1, 14).

Thus begins John's gospel. It is a stamp—an exclamation point. God gave His eternal Word living representation. It entered the world embodied in the person of Jesus Christ.

The beginning of John's gospel—particularly the first chapter —offers the reader a dizzying array of images and pictures. John seems to "pile up themes" for the reader to unpack over the course of the gospel.[2] The gospel is a dizzying blizzard of images. In fact, when Augustine wrote his commentary on this text, he called it "incomprehensible" and suggested that "it isn't read in order to be understood, but in order to make us mere human beings grieve because we don't understand it."[3] To paraphrase, God gave us this passage to completely blow our minds.

One of these themes commences immediately—the concept of "the word." Interestingly, both the book of Genesis and John's gospel begin with "In the beginning." It is as though John is picking right up where Genesis 1:1 ended. And, like Genesis 1:1, John's gospel begins with a "word."

What a fascinating way to begin one's telling of the life of Jesus. It is as if John is retelling the creation story with a twist. John, of course, knew what he was doing, as did the Holy Spirit who inspired him. John speaks of Jesus as *ha logos*, meaning "the Word." This was an important concept in the ancient world for the Greeks and the Stoics. In the ancient world, the *logos* was seen as a kind of divine power that pervaded and ordered all things, a force that undergirded all rational and moral life. It was a kind of organizing principle behind all that existed.

This would have been a foreign concept for many Jews who understood the world as created and sustained by a personal God, not by some abstract force such as *ha logos*. "Read the Torah!" a pious rabbi of the time might say. "God is not a principle; God spoke everything into existence!" And he'd be right, but notice John's inspired language here. The *logos* is not an "it." It is a "he."

John says that this one, Jesus, was the Word. The power behind the world is not an abstract principle; it is a person. If you want to see God, look at Jesus. He is the exact representation of God.

The incarnation says that God is coming to restore and redeem the world He spoke into existence. I love how Ernst Fuchs translated John 1:1 years ago: "In the beginning was the Yes, and the Yes was love and love was the Yes."[4]

This is why Jesus, in the words of many throughout church history, is what God has to say to the world. For when God wanted to speak to the world, His primary mode of communication was not a tweet or memo or message in a bottle. God, in His ultimate form of communication, does not send words, but *a* Word— Himself. If God wanted us to merely have words on paper, Mary would have written a book, not have a baby.

God saved the world through an actual person, not through a set of principles and ideas. Principles are what happen when words become more words. The Word never became more words—the Word became flesh. God doesn't save through principles. God saves through coming as the living Word.

Jesus the Conversationalist

And that living Word spoke a lot of words. We could observe many things about Jesus' conversational patterns, but let's focus on just three.

First, Jesus relentlessly spoke truth. Look, for example, at His first words in the gospel of Matthew: "Repent, for the kingdom of heaven has come near" (Matt. 4:17). His predecessor and cousin, John the Baptist, begins his public preaching ministry the same way: "Repent, for the kingdom of heaven has come near" (Matt. 3:2). Matthew's introductions to John's and Jesus' ministries are clear and to the point: they were about truth and a radical call to come back to God.

This goes against prevailing wisdom about preaching. Any preacher can remember the first time they preached. Keep it simple: open the Bible, be funny, talk about God a little, and be short. Jesus honored no such advice. He took seemingly little time to butter up the audience of the ancient world. He dug in, right away. Jesus was a radical revolutionary who called people back to the truth.

Second, Jesus spoke truth on the level of His hearer. Jesus spoke to many different kinds of people throughout His life. Yet He did not speak to everyone the same way. He always found a unique way to enter into conversations with people wherever they were.

For example, Jesus had a habit of sharing secrets of the kingdom of heaven with His disciples. He offered them intimacy that others did not enjoy. They would ask Jesus questions, and He often gave them answers (e.g., Mark 4:10–11). We call this a Q and A ("question and answer") pattern of conversation.

Other times, Jesus entered into debate and heated dialogue. In conversations with the religious leaders of His time, He typically called out dangerous and extreme prescriptions of the Jewish law. When the religious leaders gave Jesus answers, He usually answered right back. We might call this an argument or an A and A ("answer and answer") pattern of conversation.

Jesus was also fond of inciting curiosity. We see, for instance, something unique about how He interacted with the crowds—those interested people who weren't quite willing to follow Jesus but also were not religious elites with all the answers. Often, they are portrayed as wanting to see the miracles and get a free lunch. Jesus often responded to their questions with parables that seemed to confuse them even more. On many of these occasions, Jesus met their questions with more questions. We call this a Q and Q ("question and question") model of conversation.

Jesus was completely consistent about *what* He preached, but

He always adapted *how* He preached it. This, of course, teaches something deeply important about the nature of God. When God speaks to us, He always does on a level that we need and can handle. God comes down to our level. What is remarkable, of course, is that the eternal, timeless, transcendent God speaks in different ways to different kinds of people. We call this the condescending nature of God. God condescends and speaks to us in the way that *we* need.

Third, and perhaps most importantly, Jesus spent a great deal of His time with His enemies. This included both His political and religious opponents, and, in one sense, His own disciples, who eventually abandoned Him. Jesus let Judas follow Him for three years, speaking with him and listening to his questions while knowing full well that Judas would hand Him over to the authorities.

The fact that Christ even spoke to His enemies should humble us greatly. John Wesley, one of the most effective evangelists in church history, was fond of saying that "love is talkative."[5] And how true that is! We often only talk to the people we love about the things we love. Jesus extended His talk to everyone—to not only those He loved but even those who would get Him killed. His words *were* love. They were for the benefit of others, not for His own protection or interests.

Certainly, when Jesus tells us to follow His example and remember His teachings, that includes the nature of His words and speech. In so doing, we reflect the very nature of God. In fact, Jesus shared that He only did and spoke what He was given by the Father to do and say. "Very truly I tell you, the Son can do nothing by himself; he can do only what he sees his Father doing, because whatever the Father does the Son also does" (John 5:19).

Jesus reflects the Father. God in Christ comes and sits down and talks to the world—with intention. As His imitators, we should do the same. C. S. Lewis referred to our words and speech as "little incarnation[s]." When we speak something, we are putting something of ourselves into the world.[6]

Following the Conversational Ways of Jesus

To learn how to talk to others the way Jesus did, we must learn to talk to God the way Jesus did. Jesus prayed. Jesus spent time with the Father. Jesus knew who He was before God.

The Father is only recorded as speaking to Jesus twice in the New Testament: at His baptism and at His transfiguration. In both cases, they are words affirming the Father's love and the identity of Jesus: "This is my Son, whom I love; with him I am well pleased" (Matt. 3:17; 17:5).

Jesus walked in absolute security with His Father in heaven. He knew who He was because He listened to God. Without having this rock-solid identity, it is very difficult for us to maintain a Spirit-filled conversational ethic in the world.

After we've learned to talk with God, we must make it our intention to actually talk with others.

In the stories of the Gospels, Jesus always seemed to have time for a good conversation. This was true even as He prepared for His life to end on the cross, where He would save the world. Jesus had time to talk.

This stands in stark opposition to much of our culture, doesn't it? By and large, we do not have time to talk. Our lives have become cesspools of busyness. Words are exchanged at the minimum needed to keep our machines spinning, or they flood our ears at a rate we simply cannot manage. We rush off to be elsewhere with little to no time for real, relational conversation.

I'm convinced we all feel this in our gut today. We long for a certain reality or for life to be as we once knew it, but the riptide keeps pulling us out to sea no matter how hard we fight it.

There is a posture of the heart that allows for real conversational connection. If we cannot practice it by ourselves, and in the presence of God, then we won't be able to practice it in the stress and conflict of our social relationships. This is our challenge: to find ways back to being fully human. Without this, we cannot redeem how we talk.

It starts with being grounded in who we are in our relationship with God and learning to talk to God as Jesus did. Learning to do this takes time—lots of time. We do not become masters in the conversational way of Jesus the Word overnight. Learning to enter into conversation requires that we do it, regularly. As Dallas Willard once pointed out, we will never walk as Jesus walked if we do not practice what He practiced. There is no sudden or accidental Christlikeness.[7]

God is inviting us to learn how to talk to one another. But we can only do this if we are willing to learn to talk to Him again. Years ago a young agnostic woman started coming to my (A. J.'s) church with her Christian boyfriend. She wanted to meet with me, so we grabbed coffee. After swapping stories, she expressed how difficult it was for her to believe in God and accept "the whole religion thing," mostly because of some negative experiences she had with Christians years before. I empathized with her story. Finally, she asked what she should do to get over her problems with God. I gave her one piece of pastoral wisdom: start talking *to* Him. Small talk. About little things—such as the weather or how you are feeling today or how thankful you are for goat cheese. Thus began her prayer life. The young woman became a Christian not long after.

For Christians, our human conversation is made right in connection to our conversation with God. When God created the world, God spoke into the silence. He did not speak into noise.

Silence is critical. Without silence God would not have had a canvas to put something beautiful on. As Thomas Merton once said, "If we have no silence, God is not heard in our music."[8] God speaks into the silence. We must learn to be silent, too, if we want to hear Him and faithfully speak like Him. As Eugene Peterson says:

> If we talk all the time, or let others talk all the time, our ears and mouths are filled with clichés and platitudes, mindless chatter and pretentious gibberish. In silence, language is renewed. In the absence of human sound it becomes possible to hear the *logos*, the word of God that gives shape and meaning to our words.[9]

Here is the bottom line for those who would renew their conversation: all our speech is held in the speech of God. Through the example of Christ the Word, we see the relational principles that govern Christian conversation and speech. These deeply connective principles can translate into habits and—by God's power—redeem broken parts of our lives, relationships, and world.

The Holy Spirit is promised as a counselor to help us walk into the very intentions of God. As Jesus said, "When he, the Spirit of truth, comes, he will guide you into all the truth. He will not speak on his own; he will speak only what he hears, and he will tell you what is yet to come" (John 16:13). Jesus also said, when encouraging His followers not to fear when their faith comes under fire, "Whenever you are arrested and brought to trial, do not worry beforehand about what to say. Just say whatever is given you at the time, for it is not you speaking, but the Holy Spirit" (Mark 13:11).

God speaks. He speaks to the world. His speech is embodied in the living person of Jesus Christ, who gives us both an accurate picture of God and an example to follow. Because of the Spirit, we can reflect God, speak His words, embody His truth, and confidently make known the power of our faith.

Chapter 7

What Is Godly Speech?

*The tongue is also a small part of the body,
but it can speak big things.*

JAMES 3:5 NLV

The Bible makes it clear that the tongue has tremendous power.

James compares it to a rudder, which steers a whole ship. A rudder is only a fraction of the size of the boat it steers. While the rudder may have the power to steer an entire ship, someone is standing at the helm, responsible for the direction of the rudder and ultimately the ship and all the lives on it. We are in control of our tongues, and we are responsible for the direction we turn them.

James also compares the tongue to a bit in a horse's mouth. A horse is a massive, powerful animal. We even measure units of power by it (horsepower). And yet a small bit can control it.

Finally, James compares the tongue to fire. He describes the catastrophic effect a small spark can have in a forest and says that our mouths can likewise destroy a life—unleashing great chaos we cannot control.

Clearly, how we use our tongues—how we speak to one another—is important.

We have looked a great deal at how we use words in our relationships with others, and we have suggested it needs improving. But how? For what specifically are we aiming?

We are not left to guesswork. Through the various authors of both the Old and New Testaments, the Holy Spirit said a fair amount about the tongue. In fact, there are well over one hundred verses in the Bible about it. The Lord knew the impact such a small part of the body could have, and He wanted us to understand this as well. When we know where the dangers and opportunities of speech lie, we are in a much better position to engage in godly conversation: speech that is generous, hospitable, and Christlike.

There is much to say about how to practice godly speech, but we will limit ourselves to five principles. We begin with a foundational and personal truth about words and then spend the bulk of our time on words in community. We finish with reflections on the relationships between words and action, silence, and peace with God.

You Are Your Words

The foundational truth of godly speech is that it can only come from a godly heart. In Matthew 12, Jesus admonishes the Pharisees that a tree is known by its fruit. This is metaphorical speech. Jesus is comparing us to trees, saying that what we do and say is what defines us. Our "fruit" can range from being excellent to tasteless or full of worms. If words are one type of our fruit, we should care about how it "tastes" to the hearer.

In a digital age like our own, once our words are in the world, there is little hope that we can take them back. We become known for our words. It is not uncommon in our media-driven culture to see videos of celebrities or politicians caught on a "hot mic" saying something that wasn't meant for public. In many of these instances, the revelation of what someone was *actually* thinking nearly got them fired or at least culturally tarred and feathered. Whole agencies are devoted to protecting celebrities and politicians from any sort of action that might smear their image. A good deal of money is spent every year protecting the world from the actual hearts of the people we adore.

One Sunday morning, I (A. J.) was the guest preaching at a church. Having never preached at this church, I was unfamiliar with the sound system and how they wanted me to turn it off as soon as I finished my sermon. Finishing my talk—which seemed to connect greatly with the church—I went down to the front row, put my Bible on the chair, turned to the senior pastor, and whispered, "Man, I went way too long." As soon as the words left my mouth, I knew something was wrong. The hot mic picked it up for all to hear. The laughter was thick. And I have forever been known at that church as the guy who preaches for too long.

Words not only reveal who we are and give shape to relationships, but they become the evidence by which we are judged (Matt. 12:36). Famed theologian Francis Schaeffer used to say that we should all imagine wearing a microphone around our neck that records our every word and encounter. Can you imagine how that would change your conversations if every one of them was caught on a hot mic?

The truth is our hearts do not reflect what we say. Rather, what we say reflects our hearts. If our hearts are deceitful and broken, our mouths only reveal it. If they are good, our words demonstrate it.

In Matthew 12:33–37, Jesus provides a clear picture for this connection between our hearts and mouths:

> Make a tree good and its fruit will be good, or make a tree bad and its fruit will be bad, for a tree is recognized by its fruit. You brood of vipers, how can you who are evil say anything good? For the mouth speaks what the heart is full of. A good man brings good things out of the good stored up in him, and an evil man brings evil things out of the evil stored up in him. But I tell you that everyone will have to give account on the day of judgment for every empty word they have spoken. For by your words you will be acquitted, and by your words you will be condemned.

What a terrifying comment to consider. While we may be fearful of people actually catching a glimpse of who we are, be it from a hot mic or a hot-tempered moment, Jesus indicates that we should be more concerned with the judgment of God.

After someone is caught in a sin, it is not uncommon to hear them rationalize it: "I'm not the kind of person who would do that! That wasn't me! I'm not like that!" Jesus says otherwise. He takes a clear position on the reality of our harsh and empty words. When we use them, a glimpse of our heart surfaces into the world.

Knowing we are accountable for each and every word that comes from our mouths should make us stop to think about what we are saying. It should make us intentional. Even more, it should make us attend to our hearts.

Speak for the Good of Others

Because words don't exist in a vacuum but exist primarily in relationship, Scripture has much to say about how we speak to one another. The gist of its message is this: say what's good for others. This is our second principle of godly speech.

In Ephesians 4:29, Paul writes, "Do not let any unwholesome talk come out of your mouths, but only what is helpful for building others up according to their needs, that it may benefit those who listen."

Paul is inviting the church in Ephesus, and us, to consider the impact our words on others over and against our desire to say them. Listen to many of the screeds on Facebook or Twitter about the state of the world and you will find the rationale behind such words is often (though not always) to "get something off my chest." In these instances, the intent, clearly stated, is not to serve other people or even accomplish something for the betterment of society; rather it is to make the speaker feel better.

While this kind of speaking is appropriate to a degree, it is not a good ethic for healthy conversation. We don't speak merely because we will feel better for doing it but because it is better for others. Paul urges us to recognize how powerful our words are and to use them to build healthy individuals, families, and communities.

If we are to accept Paul's invitation, we must focus on the other before even opening our mouths. This is because we must know something about the other before we can effectively encourage him or her. When we know a person's strengths and struggles, we can offer authentic encouragement.

One of the disciplines we need to recapture in the West is that of verbally honoring or blessing others. Publicly blessing or honoring others creates positive space and leverages the power of words to reinforce relationships and structures within communities.

In many cultures, those worthy of honor seem to receive the respect they're due. When I (Ken) have traveled to Africa, I've noticed something really interesting in remote villages and cities teeming with energy. When someone gets up to give a speech, they name and show respect to a host of individuals before they get into their speech. I've seen it in Uganda, Burundi, Ethiopia, Kenya, and Ghana.

Now we know some of this can be political—a form of patronage—but a lot of it is cultural. Recently, I was interviewing a young Latino worship leader at our church. He took about five minutes to introduce his whole band, as well as his family, before talking about himself. Only when he started naming the remaining people who had traveled with him to our church did I realize what he was doing. He wasn't the oldest one in the room or the one who deserved all the credit for his band, so he was making sure to name everyone. Out of his cultural values he intentionally honored others.

I remember a specific fundraiser where I forgot to mention two friends—both cofounders of the organization—because of my overzealousness to engage the audience. I regret missing the chance to show two longtime friends how much they meant to me, but the night provided a good lesson. I learned that I need to slow down and be more intentional about honoring those who deserve it. I need to be intentional enough to express the respect I feel. And, if needed, I need to make a list of who needs to be honored before I speak. Even though those two friends would have been on a list of people to honor, I didn't make such a list. I was more mindful of the urgency of the event than for the potential of my words to encourage or honor others.

Words really matter. And intentional words matter all the more. Just as Jesus was intentional with His words, we as believers are called to intentionality in ours. We cannot be careless. We need to speak and be distinguished by *careful* words—literally, words that are *full of care.*

Here are a few helpful tips to promote the kind of positive speech that Paul admonishes us toward and that we desire in our relationships and encounters with others:

1. *Think about what you want to say before meeting with others.*

Prepare for the encounters you want to have. Do you want to jump into your lunch meeting or date night, simply react, and walk away wishing the conversation had gone in more meaningful and spiritual directions than simply talking about fantasy football or the latest gossip from your day at work? If so, discipline yourself to think it through before going out. In fact, bring along a note with a few things you want to discuss. Business meetings become a train wreck without an agenda, and even though they don't need to be as formal, our relational encounters can likewise lose focus if we don't tap into our deeper desires for conversation.

2. *Practice passing along good news.*

We can become habituated to focusing on the negative. We all know people who seem particularly negative, and we don't enjoy spending time with them. We also know people who seem to always be positive, and spending time with them is life-giving. Some of this positivity is born of personality, but much of it is how your brain is trained to interact with others. Our habits define us, but we also have the power to shape our habits. If we didn't, Paul wouldn't have encouraged us in the verse above to speak in a way that was helpful for building up others. Again, making notes or reminders might be a helpful way to change patterns until they become more natural.

3. Say you're sorry quickly and for simple things so you can start over.

We are trained as children to apologize when we do something wrong. Rarely is someone taught to say sorry for missing the mark on what they *wish* they would have done. Ironically, this kind of apology (e.g., "I'm sorry that I didn't start out better tonight; I really wanted to steer our conversation into a deeper place so that I could hear your heart, but somehow I was really distracted by work. Can you forgive me?") is much easier to give than when we *really* did something wrong. It also allows for a reset and the ability to pivot the conversation quickly into more healthy forms of dialogue. Plus, it's incredibly disarming and invites others to become more vulnerable with their weaknesses as well.

4. Speak to carry others' loads, not add to them.

Because we teach from the pulpit, it is easy for us to look at our own experiences to guide our preaching. Spurgeon had a beautiful principle here: Don't preach to save yourself. Don't speak in order to work out your own problems. Rather, speak something if you know it helps the other person and frees them to live more authentically before Jesus.

It is helpful to remember that we are described in the Bible as sheep, not camels. Sheep are weak, sensitive, and often very scared. We must be mindful to speak to one another in ways that will not make us more weak and scared. People are sheep, not camels. A camel's job is to carry your junk for you.

The Pharisees spoke to people as though they were camels. Jesus said of them, "They tie up heavy, cumbersome loads and put them on other people's shoulders, but they themselves are not willing to lift a finger to move them" (Matt. 23:4). In contrast, we can speak to help liberate and free each other, not further weigh one another down. This doesn't mean we shouldn't speak hard things or even process the challenges we are going through with people we trust. Of course we should. But we must use discernment in knowing when to speak heavy things to people who are already carrying much in life. Our goal in speech should be to build one another up, not unburden ourselves.

A little earlier we looked at Jesus' words in Matthew. Luke's version reads a little differently: "The good person out of the good treasure of his heart produces good, and the evil person out of his evil treasure produces evil, for out of the abundance of the heart his mouth speaks" (Luke 6:45 ESV). What is the abundance of your heart?

Luke's version underscores the need for us to be in right relationship with the Lord. We want to encourage you to explore that relationship in an effort to produce better relationships here, on earth—so that the words you speak are full of love and life.

What is godly speech? It is the manifestation of a heart that seeks to glorify God and bring about good in this world. It is speech that comes from trained patterns or habits of communication that rein in destructive talk and promote healthy conversations. Godly speech occurs when we're acting like sprinklers—taking the grace of God in our hearts and distributing it widely into the world around us, making it green.

"If anyone speaks, they should do so as one who speaks the very words of God" (1 Peter 4:11).

Words and Actions

Another principle of godly speech is that our words match our actions. This begins by remembering the words of Jesus' brother James: "Speak and act as those who are going to be judged by the law that gives freedom" (James 2:12). It is critical we learn how to not only speak but make our words echo throughout our lives. Otherwise our words are hollow, and we will be judged not only by fellow humans but by God Himself.

James addresses empty words in his epistle. He asks us to imagine being approached by someone who is in obvious need, lacking food and clothes. Do we simply smile, wave, and wish the person well? James asks what good it is to wish the person well and then to do nothing to help provide for their needs (James 2:14–16). All our speech should be run through a filter that asks:

- "Am I about to offer healing or harm?"
- "Will these words draw in or turn away the child of God who stands before me?"
- "As Christ's ambassador to this person, how can I frame my speech to be honest, inviting, and to lead him or her to a closer relationship with the source of true and abundant life?"

To be sure, our words must be accompanied by behaviors and actions that testify to Christ's transforming power in our lives.

Our actions ought to underscore the meaning of the words we speak. Without actions, words become empty. Without actions, our words may be as lovely as an iridescent bubble floating in the air, but they are void. Perhaps this is precisely what James has in mind when, later, he warns that not everyone should become a teacher: "Not many of you should become teachers . . . because you know that we who teach will be judged more strictly" (James 3:1). A teacher's vocation is about words, helping others learn through the sharing of ideas and concepts. But a teacher can easily be deceived that sharing information and knowledge is enough. It is true, after all, that most things are better caught than taught: better taken by someone's example in addition to words than words themselves. This higher standard is why James says we should all be cautious to become teachers, because teachers will be held to a higher standard by God.

Words are checks. Actions are cash. Words are what we give others with a promise that there is action behind them. But sometimes our words are more than our lives match up to. And then what happens? Our words bounce, letting others down and ultimately hurting others' trust in us. Actions are cash—they become words incarnate. Actions are words fulfilled.

Being a Christian does not mean we simply act. We must speak too. But words without action are simply a check doomed to bounce.

Silence Speaks

A fourth principle of godly speech is that it embraces godly silence.

It is a life-giving practice to give yourself times of silence—not just getting to a place where you aren't distracted by the noise of life but where you do not speak. By quieting yourself, you generously welcome the Spirit of Jesus to speak to you so that your words might be more fruitful. This intentionality of speech is also found in the wisdom of Ecclesiastes:

> Do not be quick with your mouth,
>> do not be hasty in your heart
>> to utter anything before God.
> God is in heaven
>> and you are on earth,
>> so let your words be few. (5:2)

Certainly, the advice here is pertinent to our prayers before God. But they are appropriate before people as well. In relationship, it is impossible to avoid words. Even if you are silent, words roll through your mind. They convey our thoughts.

Our Christian faith enjoins us to be generous and hospitable, and every conversation represents an opportunity to practice these virtues. But sound comes out of silence, and our efforts at godly conversation will suffer if we do not first understand how to be at peace with or handle silence.

Sometimes silence can be unwelcomed or misunderstood. Since childhood, I (A. J.) have assumed that if there is silence in conversation, there is something wrong in the relationship. Constant contact was the sign a relationship was good, and if there was no contact, something was wrong. This has created grave challenges in my adult years, especially in pastoral work. I constantly catch myself assuming if someone in the church is not responding to me, that person must be angry with me.

When I began to realize this pattern and correct it, I felt more liberated in my relationships than ever before. Now, silence can also be a sign we are in healthy relationship. We don't need to be constantly in touch for our relationship to be okay. Silence can define a relationship for months, and I can trust that the other person will, out of integrity, communicate with me if something is wrong.

If you cannot handle silence in your conversation, ask yourself: Why do I assume someone must fill the void? What in my heart makes me feel insecure when there is not constant reassurance?

We have learned that there is a drastic difference between what one might call a cold silence and a warm silence. Cold silence is the kind of silence that exists between bitter enemies—people at war with one another. This kind of silence is characterized by anger, bitterness, and resentment. But warm silence is different. Warm silence is the kind of silence that exists between two people who love and respect each other. Do you have any relationships that are so deep that you can be together and not speak and still be okay? That is warm silence.

More often than not, we allow cold silence to dictate the relationship. Warm silence is the silence of lovers who don't need to fill the space with needless noises. But cold silence is different. We should seek, in all instances, to cultivate the kind of relationships that can withstand warm silence. But because of our lack of trust and social capital with others, we let cold silence win the day.

Our healthiest relationships are always the ones where no words are needed for there to be loving intimacy.

That is why Paul can say we should "pray continually" when he clearly had times he was not on his knees presenting his requests before God. Prayer transcends being on our knees. For Christians,

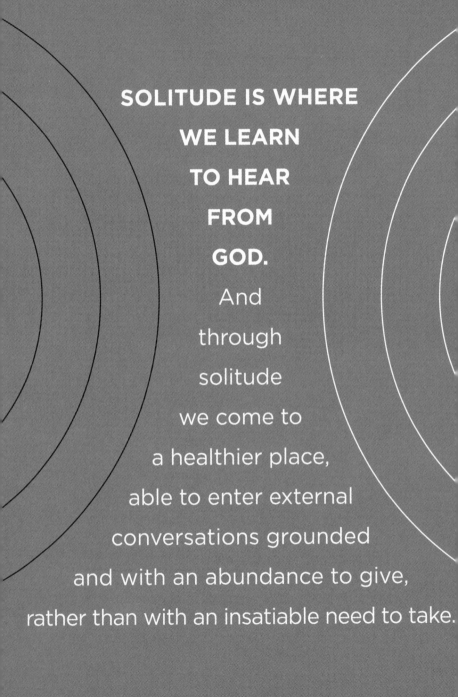

**SOLITUDE IS WHERE
WE LEARN
TO HEAR
FROM
GOD.**
And
through
solitude
we come to
a healthier place,
able to enter external
conversations grounded
and with an abundance to give,
rather than with an insatiable need to take.

prayer is a life with God and toward God. And so we can withstand silence from God and with God. We don't always need to speak to God to be connected to Him. We can be okay with silence from God. Why? Because silence from God is not always a cold silence. If God is silent, it may very well be a warm silence.

Solitude and Godly Conversation

The Trappist monk Thomas Merton once wrote, "We cannot be at peace with others because we are not at peace with ourselves, and we cannot be at peace with ourselves because we are not at peace with God."[1] What Merton helps us understand is that our relationships are, by and large, reflections of our relationship with God. They flow from one heart. If we are not at peace with God in our hearts and minds, then it will be incredibly challenging to be at peace with people in our lives.

For example, we've all walked away from a party and felt as though, somehow, despite our best intentions, our interactions that evening were more marked by our insecurities and loneliness than by our sense of security and desire to have encouraged or shaped those in attendance.

Why does this happen to us?

We are in exile. Ronald Rolheiser describes this well:

All of us live our lives in exile. We live in our separate riddles, partially separated from God, each other, and even from ourselves. We experience some love, some community, some peace, but never these in their fullness. Our senses, egocentricity, and human nature place a veil between us and full love, full community, and full peace. We live, truly, as in a riddle: The God who is omnipresent cannot be sensed; others, who are as real as ourselves, are always partially distanced and unreal; and we are, in the end, fundamentally a mystery even to ourselves.[2]

People who do not find themselves in God cannot truly find themselves in life.

I (Ken) remember in graduate school being shaped profoundly by the writings of two authors I happened to be reading at the same time. They both spoke to the issue of solitude and the need to be grounded in our conversations with God before we can truly and in a healthy way add to the conversations within our communities. Dietrich Bonhoeffer in his book *Life Together* and Henri Nouwen in his book *Reaching Out* both do a masterful job articulating the spiritual underpinnings necessary for both beginning and sustaining healthy relationships. So we've put their voices in extended dialogue together below.

Bonhoeffer and Nouwen argue that the way to escape the traps associated with the neediness of purely human love is to, in solitude, encounter God and His divine love for us in Christ. As Bonhoeffer says:

> Human love makes itself an end in itself. It creates of itself an end, an idol which it worships, to which it must subject everything. It nurses and cultivates an ideal, it loves itself, and nothing else in the world. Spiritual love, however, comes from Jesus Christ, it serves him alone; it knows that it has no immediate access to other persons.[3]

Nouwen echoes Bonhoeffer. He explains the effects our insecurities have on our relationships:

> Without the solitude of heart, the intimacy of friendship, marriage and community life cannot be creative. Without the solitude of heart, our relationships with others easily become needy and greedy, sticky and clinging, dependent and sentimental, exploitable and parasitic, because without the solitude of heart we cannot experience the others as different from ourselves but only as people who can be used for the fulfillment of our own, often hidden, needs.[4]

For Nouwen, solitude is the spiritual discipline whereby we learn to stand naked in our insecurities before God yet find love and acceptance through His grace, which creates and renews a healthy humanity within us. It is where God speaks the word we most need to hear in our most vulnerable state, such that we learn—have to learn—to embrace it. Nouwen writes:

> Instead of running away from our loneliness and trying to forget or deny it, we have to protect it and turn it into a fruitful solitude. To live a spiritual life we must first find the courage to enter into the desert of our loneliness and to change it by gentle and persistent efforts into a garden of solitude.[5]

Bonhoeffer, with his Lutheran background, had an easy time picturing the primacy of Jesus with regard to understanding the foundations of community. And Nouwen, having studied spiritual disciplines so deeply, understood that if we don't have our insecurities met through the grace of God, then we will poison community through desperately seeking to secure ourselves in ways that will never fully satisfy our loneliness.

Bonhoeffer puts our dependence on Jesus very succinctly. We are dependent on Him not only for our salvation but also for the ability to set self aside in order to empathize, love, and serve our brothers and sisters:

> Without Christ we should not know God, we could not call upon Him, nor come to Him. But without Christ we also would not know our brother, nor could we come to him. The way is blocked by our own ego. Christ opened up the way to God and to our brother. Now Christians can live with one another in peace; they can love and serve one another; they can become one. But they can continue to do so only by way of Jesus Christ. Only in Jesus Christ are we one, only through him are we bound together. To eternity, he remains the one Mediator.[6]

It is only through Jesus—through His mediating grace—that reconciliation and salvation are available to us. When our egos get in the way, it is only through quieting ourselves in "garden[s] of solitude" that we are able to grow in relationship with community, without seeking community to satisfy our needs. Rather, imitating Christ—as servants—we can love our neighbors and seek to help meet their needs instead of expecting them to meet ours.

Nouwen's counsel was to settle ourselves in prayer with God first (the internal conversation), otherwise we come to community (our external conversations) as those trying to take from it. We become destroyers of community by having no give-and-take, only an insatiable need to be filled and made secure. But when we refuse to find ourselves in Christ, we are filled with what Friedrich Nietzsche called a "Dionysian frenzy," going to and fro in a quest for the experience of intimacy. We search for an experience of intimacy with others, without ever entering into intimacy with God.

Solitude is where we learn to hear from God. And through solitude we come to a healthier place, able to enter external conversations grounded and with an abundance to give, rather than with an insatiable need to take.

More than anything, our words reflect the wellness of our hearts. This brings us to a critical conversational conviction: to speak well to others with generous hospitality, we must do the work—joyful work, if we would only do it—of being welcomed by the Father and being at peace with Him. Our prayer and conversation with God takes precedence over our words with others.

There may come a moment when you are faced with a crisis in a relationship. If you are like most people, you desire to quickly bring about resolution to the problem. Your desire for right relationship is good, and holy. But often it is important for us to stop, pause, and silently give our heart space for honest self-reflection. *What do I think about this? Where is my hurt? What sin lurks in my intentions? What are my intentions?*

We should be making sure we are in right relationship with God before we seek to address even casual matters in our lives. The condition and intentions of the heart shape our conversations more than anything else. So, next time you find yourself in a situation where you need to speak, aim to be self-aware and Christ-oriented before you let the words out of your mouth. The hard thing about words is they are like writing with pen—they can't be erased. In fact, some believe the sound waves continue on throughout the universe. This image serves only to underscore the fact that there is no taking back spoken words. May we commit to seeking security in the in-between times of solitude with God before rushing to uncap the pen of our tongue with others. For from the abundance of the heart, the mouth speaks.

Chapter 8

On Wisdom and Words

Language [is] a window into human nature.

STEVEN PINKER

In his little book *A Little Exercise for Young Theologians*, German theologian Helmut Thielicke speaks about how one does theology right.[1] Thielicke points out what he considers a travesty occurring in many seminaries. While young Christian seminary students are being taught original languages, critical Bible reading skills, and knowledge of Christian history, their love of Jesus and His church are being robbed from them.

Thielicke writes about using our knowledge of God in a wise way. He outlines two different kinds of theology in a chapter aptly titled "Sacred Theology and Diabolical Theology." With one, knowledge of Scripture and theology is used as a way to serve Jesus, people, and the church. The other, however, becomes a kind of tool for power and authority. For one, knowledge is a gift from God as a way to serve and love others. For the other, knowledge becomes about control, power, and authority. The first is sacred theology. The second is demonic theology.

More important than a controlling and religious knowledge of the Word of God is our capacity to "rightly handl[e] the word of truth" (2 Tim. 2:15 ESV). That is, we must marry our knowledge of God's Word with wisdom regarding how to use God's Word. As D. L. Moody once wrote, "The Bible was not given to increase our knowledge but to change our lives."

The topic of wisdom is not very popular in today's world.

Not too long ago I (Ken) had a vision for writing a book on wisdom. Wisdom, which has everything to do with skillful living and the pursuit of the good, the true, and the beautiful, seems to have been overlooked as a subject of study in contemporary Christian literature. We read self-help books, which are prescriptive. We read devotional books, which speak to our spiritual longings. We read spiritual-growth books, which speak to our experience and struggles and offer counsel on human spirituality. But unlike much of classical literature and philosophy, we rarely explore the subject of wisdom or its connection to human virtue as a means for human flourishing.

I shared my idea with Nicholas Wolterstorff, a friend and a professor emeritus of philosophy at Yale. He enthusiastically recommended a massive two-volume, eight-hundred-page theological treatise on human nature entitled *Eccentric Existence*. For Wolterstorff, the subject of wisdom is central to life. It grips him so much that not even eight hundred pages of academic theology could make it boring!

When I took the idea to Christian publishers, however, the response was surprisingly different. They believed the subject to be, well, a bit insipid and lacking relevance to the felt needs Christians were looking to have met in contemporary literature.

Wisdom, it seems, does not sell well in the contemporary Christian marketplace.

For Wolterstorff, who has written philosophical books on Christian education, the arts, spirituality, and justice (to name a few), eight hundred pages was just the starting point. By contrast, a 150-page book on recovering the tradition of virtue and wisdom as fundamental components of Christian thought and spirituality was considered uninteresting or irrelevant to the typical Christian audience.

My purpose is to highlight how arcane or tangential wisdom has become in the thinking of Christian pop culture. Isn't it peculiar that Proverbs, one of the best practical-advice books in the Bible, comes off as irrelevant and its primary subject matter—wisdom—as boring?

The word *philosophy* comes from the Greek *philo* (love) and *sophia* (wisdom) and simply means "the love of wisdom." What was once a bedrock subject to our understanding of humanity feels today like a lost temple from an Indiana Jones movie. Overgrown, in ruins, neglected, forgotten.

Words and Wisdom

For the ancients, "virtue" was seen as a necessary component to the good and happy life. To that end, Aristotle wrote a book on ethics entitled *The Eudemian Ethics*—a lesser known treatise than his *Nicomachean Ethics*, though regarded by some scholars as a more mature work. He begins with a discussion of *eudaimonia*, which means "happiness" or "flourishing." We don't normally think of ethics or morality in the same train of thought as happiness, do we?

But for Aristotle, as well as other ancient philosophers,

happiness was something that emanated from a life well lived. And in order to enter that life, one needed to *understand* what it was. Happiness was less associated with a feeling of pleasure or ecstasy than it was the outgrowth of virtuous living—something Aristotle would also call proper functioning. Happiness was not the result of circumstances but the reward of life well lived.

This leads us to a very important vista in our conversation. If virtue truly is important, and we arrive at virtue via understanding, then we must equally value understanding. Therein lies the importance of words; they are vehicles for understanding on the road to wisdom.

Without language—the words and the grammar of it—understanding is severely limited. Try wine tasting in the South of France—or understanding French culture and cuisine in their fullness—without knowing how to speak French or traveling with someone who does.

Here is the point: our ability to converse, to hear others, to express ourselves and receive feedback, to ask questions, or even to search for the right words to frame our thoughts and questions, are all prerequisites to learning, growing, and becoming as humans.

Theological language is the same. Our theological conversations help us probe, explore, listen, and learn about the deepest relationship and connection we can have as humans. These conversations give us unique insight into the world around us and God's intentions for it—and not only for creation but also for us as individuals and for our collaborative roles in pursuing the ends for which we exist.

We need a renewed theology of words, where words are seen as roadways to understanding and to loving God and neighbor. Rather than pragmatically defaulting to using words as a means for asserting our own individualism and self-interest or for achieving our own ends—as if we are owners of language—we must become stewards of language. Only then, in humility, can we most appreciate language and use it to serve people well. Words are not to give us power over others. Words are gifts to help us worship God and serve people.

Words, like tools and instruments, are not helpful in themselves. Words are tools to construct and build on knowledge. There are both wise ways and foolish ways to use tools. There are helpful and unhelpful ways to use instruments. A skilled worker, teacher, or scientist is one who uses the tools of his or her trade in a manner that produces quality results. Accomplished musicians make their instruments sing.

Though we understand these truths when applied to tools, we may not understand how the same rules apply to words. Yet, whether we use words as a means to investigate what it means to be human or as an expression of wise human living, words are our tools—our instruments.

We train ourselves in language (whether it is Spanish or a programming language for computers), but we seem to neglect training in the *wise* use of words. Society shapes how we use words, but it offers little help in how to use them thoughtfully to pursue what we ought to as humans. We gain the tools, sharp and ready. But we are rarely drawn aside by our teachers or parents to be shown their best use.

This is why words, speech, and communication are a major focus in the book of Proverbs. The book of Proverbs, which is referred to as "wisdom literature," underscores and illuminates how words either help or hurt as we pursue human flourishing (*eudaimonía*) in our individual lives and in the life of society around us.

Proverbs teaches us not only what to say and how to say it but also what to *refrain* from saying. If we put as much emphasis and thought into our speech as Proverbs does, it would massively reduce the dysfunction in our lives and in our society. In Proverbs, sixty-three verses discuss words and how they should be used, and seventy-seven communication in general. Here are just a few:

> Wisdom will save you from the ways of wicked men,
>> from men whose words are perverse. (2:12)

> Sin is not ended by multiplying words,
>> but the prudent hold their tongues. (10:19)

> The words of the reckless pierce like swords,
>> but the tongue of the wise brings healing. (12:18)

> Do not speak to fools,
>> for they will scorn your prudent words. (23:9)

> Gracious words are a honeycomb,
>> sweet to the soul and healing to the bones. (16:24)

It is interesting to consider *how* wisdom is portrayed in the book of Proverbs: as a female person. More specifically, as a woman who walks and talks. Wisdom has a shape and form, beauty and tenderness. Wisdom has a voice.

Proverbs 8:1–4 is a good example:

> Does not wisdom call out?
>> Does not understanding raise her voice?
> At the highest point along the way,
>> where the paths meet, she takes her stand;

beside the gate leading into the city,
> at the entrance, she cries aloud:
"To you, O people, I call out;
> I raise my voice to all mankind."

Can you picture it? A regal woman, walking with a deep nobility and calm confidence. Hers is the voice that carries truth and wisdom and expresses concern for all humankind.

The weight of this image is reinforced by the fact that Jesus Himself was "the wisdom of God" (1 Cor. 1:24). Wisdom is not an idea or a set of abstract propositions but something personified.

Wisdom calls, and she's calling out to us.

Hearing Truth

Learning how to hear truth is difficult work. We are cognitively and psychologically predisposed to only let in that which we already think or find pleasant to hear (confirmation bias, which we discussed earlier). But the Spirit of God desires to create a community of moral people who not only speak truth to one another but are also open to hearing the truth from one another.

To begin, we must recognize that biblical friendship is a unique relational context in which God envisions truth telling to take place. "Wounds from a friend can be trusted," Proverbs 27 says (v. 6). Often, the words of those we love the most hurt the most. Which is perhaps why Western culture is passively becoming a place where speaking truth to one another has become less acceptable.

Why are "wounds from a friend" important?

It is not uncommon for preachers to get letters critiquing

something they said from the pulpit. These letters take many forms, but a common one is the anonymous letter. Almost without exception, a direct relationship exists between the absence of one's name and how liberally the criticism is leveled. Where there is no name, there is no restraint. Generally, these sorts of letters are unwise to even read, let alone respond to.

A pastor might also receive an email from a leader or trusted layperson in the church. These kinds of letters, in most occasions, are different. Written, presumably, from a place of friendship and trust, there is grace and generosity in the way information is communicated.

Both critique. But usually only one makes a positive impact.

Truth telling is meant to be done, on most occasions, in the context of trusted relationship. That is why wounds from a *friend* can be trusted. You know the person. You trust the person. They love you.

On February 3, 1994, Mother Teresa delivered what was acclaimed as one of the most remarkable speeches ever delivered in Washington, D.C. She was invited to speak at a National Prayer Breakfast attended by Democratic president Bill Clinton. Standing at just five feet tall, Teresa was introduced and ushered to the podium in front of all the dignitaries. After offering some very kind and sincere introductory remarks, she immediately confronted America's long-standing tradition of being a safe place for abortions. Her message, as an outsider to America, was on a controversial national topic.

The speech had a dramatic impact on the national conversation and emotionally affected those in the room—even those who disagreed with her stance on abortion.

We don't often allow outsiders to speak to our domestic issues, and politicians usually brush aside speeches given at breakfasts like these. So why was Mother Teresa's speech so influential?

It's simple: People knew her character. She loved. No one questioned her commitment to loving the poor and vulnerable.

And that gets to a larger reality: truth telling is a sign of love and compassion. Withholding truth in a relationship is a good sign that the relationship is not as strong as one would suspect.

I (A. J.) have an acquaintance out on the east coast who has a huge circle of relationships. A few years ago he walked through a divorce. As the divorce finalized, I asked him if his friends had ever confronted him on the issue that led to the divorce. He said they hadn't. Nobody had ever said anything to him. For years his friends knew something was wrong in his marriage but refused to say anything. Why? That remains for them to know. But I know this: had just one friend discussed things with him, he might still be married today.

Not only should we be open to correction, but we need to be cultivating that openness. Cultivating openness and honesty in our speech is a form of loving our friends. Have you ever invited someone to speak truth to you? Have you ever welcomed someone into a sacred trust of friendship, wherein they feel free to say something you may desperately need to hear? Pushing past our fears of what we might hear lets us receive the love and concern of friends we otherwise would have missed.

Speaking Truth

We need people to speak truth to us, but we also must be willing to speak truth to others as both context and the Spirit allow.

In Scripture, no one was more persistent to play the role of truth teller than prophets.

Prophets were the ones who told kings that they had overlooked the widow and the orphan. Prophets wrote letters to people in power, telling them that they were not worshiping the one true God. And in many cases, they were killed. Prophets were often maligned, marginalized, and murdered. If you wanted to be well liked and to have cultural significance, being a prophet was a bad gig.

But prophets were needed. And they *are* needed. "The poor," Philip Berrigan wrote long ago, "tell us who we are. The prophets tell us who we could be." Berrigan said this is why we hide the poor and kill the prophets. It is telling that Jesus, the incarnate Lord, came as both. He embodied truth in someone who could manifest truth and demonstrate love.

Prophets are the church's immune system. Where health is missing in the Christian community with regard to how we think or converse, we ought to ask, "Where are the prophets?"

Without prophets, we are left to the mercy of every seasonal illness to which we're exposed. Christian prophecy is the power of weakness that unmasks the weakness of power. The prophet's hard words bring a better world. Truth telling is the language of Christ, who so clearly spoke of Himself as "the truth" (John 14:6). Perhaps now more than ever, prophets are in great need to revitalize the American church.

Throughout history, prophets have been marginalized in varying degrees by the church. Of course, many would say that they have to resort to using social media, blogging, and podcasting because they are no longer welcome in churches. And for that, the church must repent. A church minus prophets is a church with no immune system. Forced to use only the media, the voice of the prophet has become disconnected from localized, personal, relational communities where it is most needed and most effective.

The challenge in sharing prophetic truth is that it must be done in the right way—with wisdom. "Speak the truth in love." It's certainly a cultural cliché, and some might know that it comes from a Bible verse . . . somewhere. It's from the fourth chapter of Ephesians, where Paul writes,

> He gave the apostles, the prophets, the evangelists, the shepherds and teachers, to equip the saints for the work of ministry, for building up the body of Christ, until we all attain to the unity of the faith and of the knowledge of the Son of God, to mature manhood, to the measure of the stature of the fullness of Christ, so that we may no longer be children, tossed to and fro by the waves and carried about by every wind of doctrine, by human cunning, by craftiness in deceitful schemes. Rather, *speaking the truth in love*, we are to grow up in every way into him who is the head, into Christ, from whom the whole body, joined and held together by every joint with which it is equipped, when each part is working properly, makes the body grow so that it builds itself up in love. (vv. 11–16 ESV)

Speaking the truth in love is more nuanced than the cliché implies. It is both a *form* of existence we are all called to live into and a *means* to bring about a fuller realization of the loving community Jesus desires for His church. Put another way, speaking the truth in love both models and builds the kingdom of God.

Speaking the truth in love means sharing truth—*and yourself*—with the one to whom you speak. Blogs are a wonderful way to reach an audience, and podcasts are a fine way to carry on conversations with a tribe, but neither replace the need for us to be rooted in churches or communities where we can embody or personify wisdom and love.

Prophecy is sacred speech—or holy truth telling—designed to point us back to the path of life when individuals or society wander. Through wisdom, truth, and love, the prophetic voice stands and speaks aloud so that others may find the way of life.

Wisdom points us to how life ought to be—what it means to live skillfully and lovingly in a world that is resistant to the goodness, grace, and truth of God. Wisdom points us back to where we were meant to experience our humanity and a rich flourishing of the soul. It helps us move from introspection and return to the good, true, and beautiful.

Speaking words in a vacuum does nothing; you must garden with your words. You must live in the flower bed if you want to grow something there.

As Thielicke noted, our study of words can lead to arrogance or disengagement. It can also lead to a holy engagement in peoples' lives. As he said, there may be diabolical theology, but there is also sacred theology.

A *sacred* theology of words empowers and teaches us, as does the book of Proverbs, that words are an indispensable part of nurturing our hearts and the souls of others. It teaches us the discipline of gardening with words—of drawing from the soil of life the inherent goodness of the power of words. Of returning to the beginning, when there were just words. Words of power. Words of life. Words of truth. Words of love. Words of relationship. Words Wisdom uses as she calls out and beckons us to follow.

Chapter 9

The Mechanics of Hearing One Another

What you see and hear depends a great deal on where you are standing: it also depends on what sort of person you are.

C. S. LEWIS

Princeton University professor Uri Hasson has spent his career researching the effects of communication on the human brain. His research differs greatly from the majority of research being published in the field, which focuses on the processes occurring in a *single* subject's brain. Dr. Hasson recognizes that while we are individuals, we don't live individually. Since society and culture help to shape our minds, he focuses on brain-to-brain interaction.[1]

To do this, he looks at fMRI (Functional Magnetic Resonance Imaging) brain scans of people taken while they are engaged in different cognitive activities. Something Hasson has noted is that when one person is telling a story and other people listen to that story, the fMRI results of both the storyteller's and the listeners' brains are remarkably similar. So, while one person might be recounting something that happened to him or her, the people listening are, at cerebral and cognitive levels, sharing that experience. In terms of brain activity, there is very little difference between *telling* a story and *hearing* a story.

Hasson's research describes that while the listeners lie in the dark waiting for the story to begin, the fMRI shows dissonance between the brain waves of each person. But once the story begins, the brain waves begin to align and demonstrate a similar pattern across listeners. The synchronization of listeners' brains to the speaker's, or *neural entertainment*, as he terms it, is a predictable outcome across different sound and linguistic systems. At a brain level, we get in tune with one another through sounds.

In one experiment, a story is played for English speakers. The story was subsequently translated to Russian and played for Russian listeners. Because the speech and sound systems between English and Russian are very different, the activity in the auditory cortices differed between the two groups. However, the higher-order areas of the brains of both groups were nearly identical. Because of this, Dr. Hasson concluded that it is the *content* of the stories we hear, and not the sounds by which they are shared, that ultimately and most powerfully unites our brains. Hearing the same story creates a common ground between our brains.

Building on these experiments Dr. Hasson went on to test how preconceptions would affect the way groups "heard" or synced with given stories. In this experiment, listeners heard a story by J. D. Salinger in which a husband loses track of his wife during a party. The husband calls his best friend and asks, "Have you seen my wife?"

To test the effect of a preconceived notion, Hasson casually shared different background information with the subjects before playing the story. He told one half of the group that the wife was having an affair with the husband's best friend. He told the other half that the wife was loyal and the husband was being unjustifiably jealous.

The single sentences Hasson used to set up the story had a tremendous effect on the way each group heard the story. The listeners who believed the wife was having an affair shared the same higher-order responses across the group. Meanwhile those who believed the husband was simply jealous also shared similar higher-order responses, but they were different from the previous group. Not only were the feelings of the two groups different, but the study shows that their actual brain states were different as well. In this way, the study demonstrated the powerful effect that preconceived notions, or biases, have on us at the very deepest of levels.

Hasson is now a passionate and concerned teacher who warns about our susceptibility to bias. His research leads us to ask some important questions, such as, What happens when we watch only conservative news networks? How does that shape our interpretation of what we see in culture? Or, if we watch only liberal news, How does that shape our opinions of those who think differently from us?

Bias shapes our ability to hear truth or find common ground with others in society. A deeply relevant question to us in modern culture is why we tend to expose ourselves regularly to sources that confirm and deepen certain beliefs we hold.

It is also possible—in light of this research—to see the powerful role words of stereotype might play in the development of children and how such words shape a child's view of different people groups when they are older. In many respects, the words we hear shape our brains and ultimately color our interaction with the outside world.

If our preconceptions so deeply shape our ability to understand the words of another, how do we work around these in order to have mature and productive conversations? This chapter explores how bias divides us from one another and what we can do to work against our bias and toward unity.

Common Language, Common Values

Preconceived notions—or prejudices—are demonstrated to have the power to divide people. The more a group shares language, values, and biases, the more united they are. And the more entrenched those elements are, the more divided that group is from anyone who opposes what they share. As the saying goes, "Birds of a feather flock together." Our biases lead to tribes.

A tribe is a group that shares the same language and culture as distinct from those around them. You belong to *this* tribe, and not the *other* tribe, when you would self-identify or align yourself with one group of people and not the other. We all have tribes. No one is tribeless. For example, if we go to the Deep South and talk about the North—or Yankees—we will find that, by and large, we will get a certain common response, because many Southerners are linked by preconditions that come with living in the South. The same might be said of the Northwest, where we both live. There is a certain "lifestyle" and culture that shape how people hear and respond to others.

A common mission or purpose is often the unifying principle drawing a tribe together. A common mission is also the foundation on which friendships are built and maintained. C. S. Lewis talked about this extensively in his book *The Four Loves.* Lewis writes, "The typical expression of opening Friendship would be something like, 'What? You too? I thought I was the only one.'"[2]

This is how friendship is born and tribes are formed. When we engage in conversation, we create a space where relational interaction happens. Connecting with other people is generally easier when the conversational space is on common ground. Strangers, who might otherwise have little to discuss, are able to talk at length when the topic captures their collective imagination or interest. Contrast this with people who approach the conversational space with differing opinions, disparate interests, or opposing points of view, and such space can become muddied by argument, defensiveness, or condemnation. So we instinctively form tribes to increase our comfort and sense of solidarity and to avoid conflict. We insulate ourselves from one another.

Even for topics both parties may find interesting, our biases often contribute to different points of view. We all show up wearing a certain set of lenses that skews the way we see things.

Public speakers contend with a unique challenge in this regard. They engage in what is usually a one-sided "conversation," in which they share their thoughts and there is little opportunity for an equal exchange of ideas. In an audience of fifty, there are fifty different lenses through which the words of the speaker are parsed.

In many ways, social media is similar to a filled auditorium where the audience listens and has little opportunity to respond. While social media ostensibly provides the audience a place to respond, seldom is there a thoughtful, gracious exchange of thought. Instead, everyone is speaking, while no one is listening.

Social media is ill-equipped for dealing with bias or preconditions. Tweets, status updates, and the like are aimed at what is, in some sense, an amorphous and faceless audience. And, since they are usually dropped into existence without any prior dialogue, there is no good mechanism for first attempting to draw the listener in so he or she is in a position to receive the message being posted or shared in the spirit in which it is intended.

We find the same problem in today's churches. As churches have grown larger, and more and more congregants avoid ongoing commitments to small groups or other ministries, there is less dedicated space and time to build shared values. It has also grown harder to question our assumptions or build resiliency that allows us to stay in conversations in which we might have disagreements. Enduring hard conversations long enough is the precursor to building deep relationships and redeeming broken ones. Much of spiritual life grows slowly in time—like plants, an image Jesus was fond of using.

Tilling the Soil

Because our lives are so full, we have little time to process what is happening to us—let alone what others are sharing with us. I (A. J.) had a conversation with a military admiral who had served in both World War II and Vietnam. He told me that PTSD rates in Vietnam were astronomically higher than they were in World War II. Certainly we were much more attentive to and aware of PTSD after Vietnam. But he shared a theory with me. When soldiers returned from World War II, they had to come back on a very long transcontinental boat ride. This didn't happen in

Vietnam. Soldiers from Vietnam could be on the battlefield one day and fly back to their hometown within twenty-four hours.

My friend said he thought the difference between the two was simple: one group had time to process; the other did not. Whether his theory is accurate, we're not in the position to determine. But the idea of time to process, of rest, Sabbath, and time to grieve certainly has explanatory power and resonates with many of the biblical rhythms of healing prescribed for God's people.

Our hearts and minds often don't have space to process. Sadly, we seldom make space for what we should. In 2014 a study by the University of Virginia looked at how the modern person incorporated silence into his or her life. They asked all the participants one single question: Would you rather have fifteen minutes of silence for your thoughts, or would you prefer to be shocked by a strong electrical current for a few seconds? What the researchers found was surprising: 67 percent of men and 25 percent of women preferred to be shocked.[3]

Having time to process is important. As is listening. And quiet. And solitude. Especially for the person who seeks to follow Jesus.

I particularly like the way the art of listening is described in the *Yes, And* book mentioned earlier: "Deep, practiced listening is really a form of meditation. It is a skill that enables you to turn off the judgment part of your brain and allows you to interact with individuals and groups in a seamless way."[4]

Just as listening is a skill, so is speaking in a way that's fitting to your hearer. A speaker needs to consider the audience if he or she wants to be understood. Words, in essence, are the bridge between the speaker and the listener, and if the speaker cannot construct a sturdy bridge, the meaning conveyed by the words cannot reach its destination, the listener.

Consider the three components of communication: speaker, listener, and meaning. If words are the seeds a speaker sows, then the listener is the soil. Jesus draws upon this idea in the parable of the sower. In fact, several times in the Gospels, Jesus accuses people of having ears to hear but never hearing. They *hear* the words, but they are not *listening*. They cannot receive the meaning. The seed falls on the ground, but because of the preconditions—or the state of the heart—it never penetrates the soil in a manner that would allow the seed's potential to be realized. It won't grow.

This is also why the teacher in the book of Proverbs counsels us to "not answer a fool according to his folly" (26:4). By this, he means that the correction or advice you might offer such a person will fall on deaf ears or sterile soil.

While we cannot control how we are received, we can certainly help our cause. One way is by seeking common ground. Communicating isn't just about the content; it's also about getting aligned with the *other*. As people who ultimately long for relationship—for dialogue—we must engage the hearts of listeners first.

Whether as a husband and wife, family, church, or community, trying to become united in purpose—or one in spirit, as Paul would say—means that a lot of our communication hinges on grace, permission, and trust. These things usually must exist before we enter into difficult conversations with success. This means we'd do well to spend as much time tilling the soil as we spend sowing seeds. As Dr. Hasson's research showed, context has a profound impact on how we hear and react to stories. Next time you consider a difficult conversation, think, *What is the relational context for this conversation? Is there something I could do to till the soil?*

Next to prayer, listening is perhaps the best way to create a positive context for conversation. Listening forces us to exchange hats with others, to walk in their shoes. When we exchange hats, we develop empathy and understanding. Then we can more tenderly voice our concerns or offer our advice. We become like a doctor, attuned to the sore spots and thus more adept at treating them. You can never go wrong with listening, but you can rarely go right without it.

Seeing with New Lenses

The Holy Spirit leads us to see things we may have missed before.

Immediately after the Spirit of God falls on the church in Acts 2, Peter goes on a walk through Jerusalem. There, he sees a man who has been brought to the temple gate day after day for years. Peter had probably seen this man a thousand times before. But this time, something changes. When the man asks for money, Peter looks down and says, "Look at us!" (Acts 3:4).

Why did he want the man to look at him? Perhaps it is because the man was accustomed to feeling invisible (like the man who threw himself off the Golden Gate Bridge). But Peter wanted him to know he wasn't invisible. The man looks up, has an encounter with Jesus, and is changed. It all began with Peter seeing him.

The Spirit of God changes the way we see things. Alexia Salvatierra, Lutheran minister, author, and consultant, is a national leader in the areas of poverty and immigration. She once made a statement about the "economics" of relationship: "Relationships are what life is about, and relationships trade on the currency of language and communication."[5] If this is true—and we believe it is—then the Spirit of God also helps us *see* relationships differently.

Based on our experiences, language can never be viewed as existing in a vacuum. That is, we cannot talk about communication without also talking about cultural influence. For example, the Tagalog language of the Philippines has two distinct words for *we*. Where English has only one *we*, the word *tayo* includes the listener, and the word *kami* excludes the listener. *Kami* would be a near equivalent to "my tribe."

Spanish is another language without a one-to-one meaning across translation of a particular word. Spanish has no word for *compromise*. This doesn't mean compromise doesn't exist in Spanish-speaking cultures. As Alexia worked with Latino couples in marriage counseling, she learned the best replacement for the concept of compromise is "*concertar*," which means "coming into harmony." To be in collective harmony, each person must really hear the other person's heart and then be willing to align generously with them. Alexia noted, "Reaching halfway [a compromise] is what we do in business, not in relationship."

The mechanics of any given language—the words, morphology, and grammar—are not the only things separating different cultures. Cultures communicate differently.

While working in the Black and Latino communities of South Los Angeles, Alexia observed that each of the groups resolved conflict uniquely. The only way these two groups would be able to work together well required an understanding of this difference.

Alexia, who has been a community organizer and peacemaker in these neighborhoods for decades, explained that African Americans in her neighborhood tend to deal with conflict in its early stages. While all in "good fun," they make their points forcefully. When conflict is handled in the stage when things are still free and easy, there typically isn't any serious anger or hurt among the parties. However, most Latinos (specifically, Mexican and Central American people) consider this same kind of expressive communication rude. In Latino culture, such forceful communication is tantamount to throwing down a gauntlet. Thus, what makes for a spirited debate among African Americans are fighting words for Latinos. Instead, Latinos get very quiet and want to discern what the actual threat or desire is. If things go on too long, they tend to quietly get very fierce and very serious.

When the groups understood and kept in mind the differences in their methods of conflict resolution, their interactions changed—they understood they had been talking past each other. It took *getting to know the other* before they could communicate effectively.

Alexia summed it up well:

> We need to understand that relationship is not automatic. It must be built, not assumed. Even in the body of Christ, you have to live *in* to it. While the framework and potential are present, relationship doesn't happen until you build it. And, it is not built by sitting across the table but by engaging in joint missions and common work that matters to you. Prayer is the simplest form of joint mission. Joint mission creates a context for building healthy relationships where effective communication follows.

Becoming Culturally Bilingual

One of the premises of this book is that we need healthy and effective communication if we want good, healthy relationships. If we want to love our neighbor in a globalized world, this means, perhaps more than ever, we need to become culturally bilingual. This doesn't necessarily involve crossing national boundaries. In the United States, we need only go as far as the next state, city, or sometimes, just the next door.

We need to be able to understand different cultures.[6] Paul had a missionary's heart. He was often seeking to build bridges to the various cultures of his day. In one letter, he wrote, "When I was with the Jews, I lived like a Jew to bring the Jews to Christ. When I was with those who follow the Jewish law, I too lived under that law. Even though I am not subject to the law, I did this so I could bring to Christ those who are under the law" (1 Cor. 9:20 NLT). How comfortable are we doing likewise?

As Christians, we know we are called to love people. It is far easier to love people when we know them, understand them, and are working with them—not against them. Belinda Bauman, a friend of ours who leads a movement of women fighting global injustice centered on gender violence, has a PowerPoint presentation she uses to train people for cross-cultural engagement. In it she has six or seven principles common to both secular and ministry approaches to cross-cultural communication. She points out, first, that love is "culturally defined,"[7] and the better we understand a culture, the better we can love, particularly regarding the following concepts:

- Self: Does the culture operate as a set of individuals, or does it function as a group, where the interests of the group prevail over those of the individual?

- Communication: Is meaning conveyed by words (direct) or nonverbal cues (indirect)?

- Power: Is power understood as equality among members of the group, or is there a prescribed hierarchy?

- Interaction: Is the cultural interaction primarily task-oriented, or are relationships between members of the culture more important than tasks? Is *who* more important than *what* or *when*?

While most cultures exist on a continuum between each concept pair, to communicate across cultures in a relevant way it is important to understand your native cultural assumptions and those of the community you are entering into dialogue with.

Author Duane Elmer puts this concept succinctly and brilliantly:

> We are called to love all people. But can I truly love someone I do not, at least to some measure, understand? Love requires at least some understanding of its object. . . . When we truly love others, we love them in their own context, in keeping with the way they define love. We can't express love in a vacuum.[8]

True love cannot exist apart from understanding. A level of self-awareness and others-awareness is essential.

I (Ken) remember attending some smaller, culturally diverse gatherings of several dozen people, where I was only one of two or three white people. As a verbal processor, when there was a lull in the conversation, I took the opportunity to jump in and freely share my ideas. I didn't understand the different cultural dynamics in the room, and I hadn't taken the time to listen or understand how a multicultural group needs to function so that everybody's voice is heard. I was grateful that someone took the time to gently point this out afterward. She explained that being the white man in the room wasn't just a description of my physical appearance; it also pointed to underlying cultural assumptions, the confidence that comes with them, and the degree to which I am accustomed to inserting my voice as regularly or as often as I want.

I am still growing, and I am still learning, but now—more than ever—I am realizing there are many different ways in which cultures orient themselves to conversation, speech, and expression. As I seek to live in the broadest and healthiest community expression possible, I must continue developing the skills of leading as well as listening.

In an age of globalization, and in an era where America and the church are wrestling with the long-term effects of racism, understanding the role of voices (the people we platform, pursue, engage, and listen to) is a much-needed part of our conversational and educational ethics.

It is important to remember that in order to love others, our love needs to connect with them. We need to love in such a way that others *feel* our love. If they don't, we have missed the mark. Galatians 6:2 tells us we are to "bear one another's burdens, and so fulfill the law of Christ" (ESV). To carry my sister's burdens, I must first know what burdens her. To mourn with my brother, I must first know what grieves him. With this awareness, I want to carefully choose what I say, how I say it, and when I say it.

To love one another, we must first hear one another.

Chapter 10

The Unity of the Church

*Come. Let us have some tea and
continue to talk about happy things.*

CHAIM POTOK

In 2003, sociologist Philip Slater wrote an article called
"Connected We Stand." Within it, he talks about organizations
and political ideologies that cause people to separate and divide—
he calls these two cultural systems "the Culture of Division and
the Culture of Connection."[1] The difference, Slater suggests, is
that the first seeks to cross boundaries, while the second seeks to
undermine and dissolve them. In North America, there generally
seems to be a popular notion that if we could just get together and
talk about the issues, then everything would work out well. This is
a naive approach, one that ultimately does not take seriously the
important and fundamental ways in which people disagree.

The reality is that it's not just hard for us to talk together; it's
hard for us to do something as simple as eat together.

Members of A. J.'s church, Theophilus, eat together each and every week. Such a rhythm can be incredibly difficult, and the commitment to this has been challenged as the church has grown. They have learned one thing about meal sharing: it scares some people. Ironically, for the consumer Christian who is looking to come, sit in the back row, and watch, the meal is hostile to what they want. The meal can be intrusive, scary, and difficult. When you sit down at a meal, you are forced to share food and space with people you don't necessarily understand or want to make the effort to understand.

It does not require a miracle for a church of Democrats to hang out together. Nor does it require a miracle for a community of Republicans to eat together. Neither of those communities requires God's reconciling presence. Getting Democrats and Republicans to learn to love, serve, and care for one another requires not only the grace of God but a miracle. The community of Christ is not built on personal preferences. It is built on Christ, who has little or nothing to do with individual tastes whatsoever.

Just as the Bible imagines words and speech as deeply holy and inspires us to imitate the conversational ministry of Jesus, it also places our work of communication in a communal context. We are not isolated speakers. Rarely, if ever, are we solitary voices crying out in the wilderness. Rather, every Christian is part of an interconnected organism that ought to speak one Word in many voices.

Our most common name for that speaking, praising, prophetic, praying organism is *the church*.

Pentecost and Babel

Many theologians trace the "birthday" of the church to the day of Pentecost described in Acts 2. But there is actually an earlier, foundational story that launched the whole Pentecost tradition, and it's found nowhere near Acts. It's all the way back in Exodus.

It was fifty days after the miraculous deliverance of the Jewish people (hence the word *Pentecost*, meaning "fiftieth") when Moses ascended Mount Sinai to receive the law of God for the people below. The text tells us that as Moses is receiving the Ten Commandments atop the mountain, it shakes with an earthquake. Soon he descends, only to find God's people worshiping a golden calf—the religious idol of the Egyptians, from whom they'd just been freed. God pours out anger on the people for their idolatry, and on that day three thousand Israelites are killed. This was a painful lesson but an essential one.

Now flip forward to the story of Pentecost in the New Testament. Jesus had died just fifty days earlier, then ascended. The church, told with His parting words to wait in Jerusalem for "power," is doing just that—waiting, in the upper room of a house in downtown Jerusalem. The place is "suddenly" shaken by a wind, akin to an earthquake. The church then receives the Spirit of God. Almost immediately, Peter stands up to preach in the middle of Jerusalem, which is jam-packed with people celebrating the first Pentecost. At this Pentecost, as Peter preaches about Jesus, the good news is received. Luke tells us three thousand people are saved.

Interesting. The inspired Scriptures are up to something. In the first Pentecost, only Moses goes to the upper place. In the second, the whole church ascends to the upper room. In the first Pentecost, there is an earthquake. In the second, a rushing of the winds of heaven. (Both events shake the people of God.) The first Pentecost happens fifty days after the death of the Passover Lamb and the killing of the firstborns in Egypt. The second takes place fifty days after the death of the firstborn of God, who is the Lamb that takes away the sins of the world. The first Pentecost shows God's people acting like worldly people. In the second, the world is becoming the people of God. And finally, in the first Pentecost, three thousand are killed. In the second, three thousand are saved.

The Spirit-filled Pentecost in Acts 2 is the reversal of the dark, idolatrous Pentecost in Exodus. Something powerful happens when the Spirit of God falls on His people. Pentecost is the great reversal. Yet this is not the only reversal. Consider, as well, the story of Babel.

At Babel, because of the idolatry of humanity, God confuses the language of the people of the world. This is the biblical explanation for why there are so many languages. Since Babel, humanity has struggled to be in conversation with one another.

But something interesting takes place, again, in the story of Pentecost in the book of Acts. When the Spirit falls, the church suddenly has the supernatural ability to speak in the tongues and languages of all the people nearby. The bewildered crowd says, "How is it that each of us hears [the gathered believers] in our native language?" (Acts 2:8).

The Pentecost of the church's founding reverses the first Pentecost that marked the giving of the law of Moses. And Pentecost reverses Babel. Now, by virtue of the Holy Spirit, the church is sent into the world to spread the gospel to each and every people group of the world in their own tongue.

Babel has been undone. Pentecost is Babel backward.

In Acts 2 we are watching the church learn to speak. Pentecost is the birthday of the church, and these are her first words in the post-Pentecost world. In what follows, we outline some of the ways the early church continued learning to speak, which helps us consider carefully how we speak today.

Church Talk: Truth in Community

When we look at the early church, we discover that truth telling was always done in the context of community. Truth and community went hand in hand. In his iconic examination of the early Christian church, *Paul's Idea of Community*, Robert Banks writes about Paul's understanding of the community of faith. For Paul, when one was saved into Jesus, he or she was saved into that community.[2] There was truly no concept for Paul that one could follow Jesus *outside* of the community of faith. Roger Olsen writes, "There is no hint of Lone Ranger Christianity in the New Testament; there is no suggestion that a person can be vitally united with Christ and growing spiritually apart from the church."[3] And this complete identification with the larger body carried implications for dialogue.

To be in the truth was to be in the church. Look at Paul's language in Romans 16. Paul writes what is often overlooked as a kind of laundry list of greetings and names—it personally mentions some *thirty-eight* people by name. The list is profoundly diverse and lists both men and women, urbanites and rural folks, servants and government employees. These people were the church in Rome, but remarkably, *Paul had yet to go to Rome.* Consider the brilliance of that. Paul knew the names of thirty-eight people whom he'd most likely never met.

Paul went to great lengths to get to know people. In the book of Galatians, we find that Paul describes what it was like to join the Christian community. After his conversion, he went to Jerusalem to meet the apostle Peter, spending fifteen days with him there. As Paul describes the experience, he uses the word *historeo*, which often refers to "history." But it was more personal than that. As German scholar Friedrich Buchsel argues, that word means something along the lines of "visit in order to get to know."[4] Eugene Peterson aptly translates it as "swapped stories."[5] The point is that Paul and Peter are not merely talking history; they are getting to know each other. They took time to be in each other's lives. "On and on" they went, Peterson continues, "fifteen days of story-telling as they got to know one another as brothers in Jesus, discovering intimacies of the Spirit as they opened their vulnerable hearts to one another."[6]

For Paul, community was the context wherein the follower of Jesus ought to speak truth. It is, of course, completely possible to do community *minus* truth. Robert Wuthnow wrote a great book in 1994 called *Sharing the Journey*, in which he has shown that most small-group structures in America are largely about the sharing of feelings, *not* the telling of truth.[7] Within these small groups, people find their social needs met in place of where they used to find them—in the family. The problem with substituting a small group for the intimacy of family relationships, of course, is that in these groups people create space for emotional needs but not the healthy, occasional confrontation that true and honest community invites and demands. The sharing of feelings is, indeed, an important aspect of community. However, when members of a small group have truth spoken to them or are held accountable for their actions and behavior, they are likely to move on to another group where there is no judgment and they can simply be supported emotionally.

Equally, is it possible to do truth *minus* community? So much of the modern American structure of podcasting is built on this premise. We listen to our favorite preachers but are not living out this truth in a community.

Truth is meant for community. And community is meant for

truth. This is absolutely central; if we abandon community, then we often do not have opportunities for truth telling to be done in love, and our truth telling often ceases to look like that of Christ. As pastors, one of the most difficult aspects of the way we do community in the church is that if we were to "correct" or "truth tell," we are almost certain the person will leave. While he or she may not leave the church, that individual will likely leave our community and go worship God with a different community down the street.

This is almost exactly why the practice of church discipline is impossible in American church culture. When things get hard, we can go to the church down the street. We posture ourselves in such a way that although we have the truth and the church needs the truth we have, we do not take our responsibility seriously to help people live it out. This is represented by "truth bombers." Truth bombers drop truth and then leave. They quietly step out of the scene to let others make sense of it, grapple with it, and apply it. Meanwhile they steer clear of the mess.

I think of a story in one of John Grisham's novels, *The Testament*, in which a character goes on a mission trip and, in an effort to build relationships, waits six years to tell his first Bible story. His instincts were right; the indigenous people did not want to hear what he had to say until they knew he would never leave them.

People's receptivity to truth is largely connected to the clarity of our love and long-term commitment to them. Nobody wants truth shot at them from the outside with no personal commitment. Truth is shared best in loving relationship. Jesus never dropped truth bombs and then abandoned people to their own devices. Jesus, instead, gave truth and gave Himself. Or, to be more precise, He gave Himself, and in so doing gave truth. "I am the truth," Jesus said. He was completely truth telling and loyal.

The church is called to the truth of Jesus. We are often tempted to respond to all sorts of other calls. But our primary calling is to Jesus and the truth He bore to the world. When you read about Roman conquests during the Roman Empire, you'll find the Romans had a very strategic way to condition new subjects. When they would capture a particular land or people group, they would pacify them with two things: the now-cliché "bread and circuses."[8] First they would give free bread to all the people. Then they would build a colosseum to entertain them. This policy had a powerful way of stifling any dissent.

Too often, even the church puts too much emphasis on entertaining Christians and simply meeting felt needs. But we are not called to pacify the world or the church with entertainment. The church is about truth. Truth that is at times hard, painful, bloody, and very disturbing.

But without truth, we cannot be set free.

Church Talk: Unity through Difference

Finally, we must recognize the great diversity of the early church. Snap back to that remarkable Pentecost moment in Jerusalem. There were Gentiles and Jews, Greeks and Romans, men and women, slaves and slave owners—the diversity of the early church was staggering. How was this possible? How could this be?

I would argue that this kind of diversity was only possible because there was such strong unity around the person of Jesus.

Shared experience makes for good community. In Luke 1, Elizabeth goes to visit Mary when they are both pregnant. Mary sings a song of thankfulness to God. In the final verse of that section, we read, "Mary stayed with Elizabeth for about three months and then returned home" (Luke 1:56). Three months? Ever just popped in for fifteen minutes and it felt like forever? Three months! Not only is this a powerful example of hospitality, but it shows the power of shared experience. They both were pregnant. They both had been caught up in the kingdom of God. They were kin, yes, but they were kindred spirits, and that served as the basis for their joy in each other.

Although the church was united around the person of Jesus, there was still disagreement within it. We see multiple occasions of this. Paul and Barnabas disagree over missiological concerns. Two women in the church of Philippi—Euodia and Syntyche—are told to agree in the Lord. And John airs his concerns over an individual named Diotrephes, "who loves to be first" (3 John 1:9). And there are more. Disagreements are not only an everyday reality, but they are included in the pages of Scripture.

The fact that the church could handle disagreement speaks to the strength of the community. Stanley Hauerwas says:

> Good communities are spaces where people love one another enough that they're not afraid of disagreements. . . . People that are together to be together, that's just another name for hell. . . . You never are together to be together; you're together because you have something you want to do.[9]

This is maybe one of the hardest things about community—engaging our differences.

The community of Jesus is that place where we come together to be one in Jesus, but the rest of life we break into much smaller tribes. Our lives reveal a kind of pronounced *conversational gentrification*, where we are sanitizing our lives from those of theological, ideological, and political difference. Ominously, we spend our lives curating spaces that have as minimal conflict as possible, doing everything in our power to relate only to people who look like us. Rather than compassionately loving the other, our neighbors, the refugee, the religious—those people who bring with them the certainty of difference and otherness—we self-select a community that offers little disruption to our comfort. We insulate ourselves from discomfort. We live in bubbles. And we love those few who will never pop our bubble.

Like Hauerwas, C. S. Lewis considers this a sort of hell. In *The Four Loves* he writes:

> To love at all is to be vulnerable. Love anything, and your heart will certainly be wrung and possibly be broken. If you want to make sure of keeping it intact, you must give your heart to no one.... Wrap it carefully round with hobbies and little luxuries; avoid all entanglements; lock it up safe in the casket or coffin of your selfishness. But in that casket—safe, dark, motionless, airless—it will change. It will not be broken; it will become unbreakable, impenetrable, irredeemable. The alternative to tragedy, or at least to the risk of tragedy, is damnation. The only place outside Heaven where you can be perfectly safe from all the dangers and perturbations of love is Hell.[10]

In hell, everyone agrees. There is totalitarian unanimity. But love—and most noticeably, God's love—are not welcome. There may be no danger from vulnerability, but there is also no comfort from love.

We wrongly conceive of the church as a place where everyone needs to agree with one another on everything. There indeed is a shared core of what it means to be a Christian. This can be identified in a reading of the Nicene and Apostles' Creed. There are certain beliefs we must share to be called Christians. Beyond that, there is room for diversity and disagreement. We would even suggest that trying to create church cultures of unanimity around all theological, all political, or all ideological issues is a reflection of secular unity rather than biblical unity. In the New Testament church, there simply were too many differences for us to seek to create homogenous churches that are the same in all things. Our goal should be biblical unity, not a secular notion of unity.

And with that it should be recognized that even God's people in the Old Testament were not one tribe. They were twelve tribes, all worshiping the same God. Unity, not uniformity, is essential. Jesus prayed in John 17 that His church would be one as He and the Father are one (v. 11). Real unity does not mean we have organizational unity. That is, we may be in different organizations and denominations and still be unified. Different denominations and tribes might actually be part and parcel of God's divine plan to see every tribe and tongue worship the Lamb of God. As Paul says: "One Lord, one faith, one baptism" (Eph. 4:5). He never says one organizational structure or one perfect theological system.

Have you ever noticed that in Revelation 21, heaven is described as having no sea? It's no random detail. In Scripture, the sea is a demarcation between dry lands. It divides. There are whole people groups on islands that have no relationship to the rest of the world.

In the new world, we will be one island. No divisions, no demarcations, no denominations. We will come together and worship at the throne, and the Lamb of God will be at the center of it all. We will love the same Lord *as we are.*

The church ought to be a community with truth in its mouth. Metaphorically, we "eat" it together during our gatherings, experiencing the nature and unifying work of Jesus. Then we speak it, our words formed and tempered by the same potent love and creative power that God's words had at the beginning. Our community life is not truth *and* love, but truth *in* love. We speak what we have heard. Or at least we ought to.

Chapter 11

The Art of Winning People Back

*Grace must find expression in life,
otherwise it is not grace.*

KARL BARTH

When I (Ken) began to seriously follow Jesus in college, I remember being taught how to go and look for a "good" church. My campus minister, an older pastor who took his job of shepherding his students very seriously, would recount again and again that there were three marks of a healthy church: the Word rightly preached, the sacraments rightly administered, and church discipline rightly practiced.

It seemed fair enough, and it resonated with some of what I remembered from the Baptist churches I grew up in.

So I took that definition. I evaluated churches on their Bible teaching, cared a bit less about how they did baptisms or the Lord's

Supper, and made sure that they judged sin and took seriously the mistakes of their leaders.

In fact, this definition became so baked into me that I taught it again and again for around a decade when I pastored my own groups of college students.

I've come to realize that I'm not alone. I talked about this on a recent Sunday and asked people to raise a hand if they had been raised with the same three marks of a good and godly church. About one-third of the audience quickly responded by putting an arm in the air.

What church discipline meant to me growing up was that the church was going to excommunicate people now and then for refusing to change direction, holding a wrong belief, or failing morally. It usually meant that these acts would be made public and that the sinner would be named from the pulpit (and certainly discussed between congregants person-to-person). I sometimes wonder if this hypersensitivity to sin, and the potential for public discipline always hanging in the air, is why so many messy people feel out of place or judged in the church.

Are these the hallmarks of the church Jesus intended for us to have? Did Jesus leave us with mechanisms to simply call out sin or to jump in and repair brokenness? What if the love Jesus intends for us—and wants as a testament that we are indeed true followers of Him—is something that needs to be fought for and established as we come together in difficult and redemptive conversations?

When Context Matters

Historically, church discipline was conceived from love and a desire to disciple people toward holiness. Sadly, the modern form of American discipleship has, in many respects, descended into legalism.

We have either lazy conflict resolution habits or we eschew it altogether and default to judging people we perceive to have wronged us. Either way, we find ourselves caught up with gossip, hearsay, and all manner of speech involving various parties—none of which helps work toward reconciliation.

Sometimes it seems as if we judge because God first judged us, instead of loving because He first loved us (as Scripture so poignantly encourages us). This is evidenced in our perpetuation of one of the greatest misunderstandings of Scripture in the evangelical world: our interpretation and misapplication of Matthew 18.

Church discipline is a phrase and a concept of which many of us are at least somewhat familiar. However, the primary passage for it—Matthew 18:15–20—seems to aim at something radically different from excommunication or making sure we don't let any sin persist in the church.

The parables or stories directly prior to and after Jesus' words on dealing with sin in the church give us a clear sense of how to interpret His instructions. Looking at the NIV version of Matthew 18, the section on "Dealing with Sin in the Church" is sandwiched between two passages: "The Parable of the Wandering Sheep" and "The Parable of the Unmerciful Servant." The parable of the wandering sheep is about God's *unrelenting love* for every individual He has created. The shepherd would leave the ninety-nine sheep to go seek and save the one lost. Jesus' heart for every man and woman—the wayward, the sinner, the vulnerable—comes across so clearly and tenderly in this metaphor. God is love.

The parable of the unmerciful servant is about the hypocrisy of receiving God's grace but failing to have mercy and grace for one another. In many respects it calls out the behavior of churches that, though recipients of grace, don't know how to show that same grace to others, outsiders, or sinners. These servants receive grace but dish out judgment. It pains me how familiar this probably is to many of us.

Both the passages on either side of this "church discipline" passage are about *love, grace, and relationship.*

Context matters.

Jesus' Pattern for Dealing with Conflict

So what does Jesus say in the middle of the Matthew chapter to expound on His theme of grace and forgiveness?

Here is Matthew 18:15–20 in its entirety:

> If your brother or sister sins, go and point out their fault, just between the two of you. If they listen to you, you have won them over. But if they will not listen, take one or two others along, so that "every matter may be established by the testimony of two or three witnesses." If they still refuse to listen, tell it to the church; and if they refuse to listen even to the church, treat them as you would a pagan or a tax collector.
>
> Truly I tell you, whatever you bind on earth will be bound in heaven, and whatever you loose on earth will be loosed in heaven.
>
> Again, truly I tell you that if two of you on earth agree about anything they ask for, it will be done for them by my Father in heaven. For where two or three gather in my name, there am I with them.

So let's walk through it.

First, Jesus encourages us that if an issue of division or misunderstanding cannot be reconciled between the two parties, have a group conversation with two or three others so that nothing is misunderstood.

Jesus values love and grace and unity and straightforward talk. Don't run first to others but to the one with whom you have an issue.

Second, if this doesn't work, enlarge the circle only a bit to have two or three peacemakers present. Why two or three? When He says, "so that 'every matter may be established by the testimony of two or three witnesses,'" He is pointing back to the legal principle in Deuteronomy 19:15 that says, "A single witness shall not suffice against a person for any crime or for any wrong in connection with any offense that he has committed. Only on the evidence of *two witnesses or of three witnesses* shall a charge be established" (ESV). Jesus is building on the patterns of truth finding and resolution set in the Old Testament.

Think about it. If the word of only one witness was all it took to convict someone, we could have gotten a myriad of people locked up. Our colleagues. Our teachers. Our Sunday school teacher. Anyone we didn't like. The Salem Witch Trials occurred because one young person would accuse someone, and action was taken on the word of that one witness. Crazy stuff happened. Beatings happened. Imprisonment happened. *Murder* happened. In our disagreements, Jesus intends for cool heads to prevail and for us to follow a mature process.

Third, later in the passage he affirms that if two or three people are there, Jesus will be there too. Jesus *is not* saying that where there are two or three Christians, you have a "church." I (Ken) have heard this verse misquoted more times than I can count, usually as an excuse for someone who is no longer choosing to attend a local church. "I belong to a church simply by virtue of being in relationship with a few other believers," the comment goes. By that logic, I can have church all by myself simply because I carry the Holy Spirit within me. Rather, Jesus' reference to the two or three harkens back to the idea of neutral or trustworthy witnesses trying to help resolve a heated dispute. And as encouragement, He promises that He will be with the peacemakers in the peacemaking process if it is being handled in a mature and biblical manner.

Lastly, reading on, the passage says, "If they still refuse to listen to you, tell it to the church, and if they refuse to listen to the church, treat them as you would a pagan or a tax collector."

We've often read the idea of tax collectors through our disciplinary lens and landed on excommunication. But how did Jesus treat tax collectors? For Jesus, they were simply lost sheep. The sinner was already on the outside of community, living in the consequence of their sin. His primary loving desire was to seek and save them.

Matthew 9:10–11 says, "While Jesus was having dinner at Matthew's house, many tax collectors and sinners came and ate with him and his disciples. When the Pharisees saw this, they asked his disciples, 'Why does your teacher eat with tax collectors and sinners?'" Jesus was spending so much time with tax collectors that it confused the religious leaders. Do churches that practice "good church discipline" treat sinners the same way Jesus treated tax collectors? Not in my experience.

Reconciliation must always be the driver in discipline. This North Star of discipline often gets lost, and we disconnect our actions from Jesus' commands to love and from a gospel that points us toward a God who is reconciling all things to Himself.

If Matthew 18 is about reconciliation and how communities are supposed to work through their conflict in hopeful, mature, and loving ways, where did the heavier reading of Matthew 18 come from? Where did our focus become church discipline rather than church reconciliation or conflict resolution?

The Belgic Confession

The three marks of a healthy church given to me by the college minister weren't his own. They were marks that came out of the Protestant Reformation, partly motivated in response to the abuses of the Catholic church of the day. The Reformers believed the Catholics taught the Scriptures wrongly, practiced too many sacraments, and didn't take sin and holiness seriously enough—especially coming out of the recent season of worldly Renaissance popes living openly licentious lives in the late 1400s and into the 1500s.

The three marks are found in Article 29 of the Belgic Confession of Faith, a document drafted in 1561. The beginning of the second paragraph reads:

> The marks by which the true Church is known are these: If the **pure doctrine of the gospel is preached therein**; if it maintains the **pure administration of the sacraments** as instituted by Christ; if **church discipline is exercised in punishing of sin**. [emphasis added]

From there they traveled and were codified as the Protestant faith went to the New World and established churches and denominations.

If you Google "marks of a healthy church," look at the values of church-based ministries, or look at the literature of church denominations, you will see these three marks stated outright, used as a backbone for larger lists, or implied in the verbiage. They have become for us a sort of creed.

It all seems really logical, right?

These marks might be biblical principles, but there is one biblical idea that is conspicuously absent from the list—the one command Jesus gave to His followers and the hallmark He said would set them apart and make them recognizable as His followers: love.

Love Never Ends

"By this everyone will know that you are my disciples, if you love one another" (John 13:35).

Maybe I make too much of this, but what happens when, for hundreds of years, church discipline is on our list of "marks of a healthy church" and love isn't? I find that unbelievably profound.

And what happens to our reading of passages such as Matthew 18 when we have church discipline as an active priority but not the mandate of love sitting alongside or overarching it?

Again, I'm not saying discipline is wrong. I am saying that, just like when I discipline my daughters, it has to be born of love and aimed at reconciliation. Discipline without an eye to reconciliation is masochism or sadism. In homes, we would remove children for as much.

My fear is that at times in the life of the church, the neglect of love as the hallmark of the church has led to self-righteousness and the reflex to judge too quickly, give grace too slowly, and put people out of fellowship sooner than welcoming them into it.

Wasn't the story of the woman caught in adultery just this picture?

Jesus, here is this woman.

We know what the law says and how we should discipline her.

Let's see what you say we should do with her—are you going to follow the law? Do you care about purity? Are you going to honor the holiness of God by giving her what she deserves?

These people were ready to throw stones. In our culture we don't throw stones, but we do cut with words. Jesus, after scribbling in the dirt, stands and addresses them. He defuses the situation with simple words. True words. *"Let any one of you who is **without sin** be the first to throw a stone at her"* (John 8:7).

It's His mercy and our sin that causes us to drop our stones—to swallow our hurtful words before we bludgeon others with them.

They were asking the wrong question. Love, not discipline, is what defined Him—and what should have defined them.

The church is unfortunately famous for shooting its wounded. C. S. Lewis said, "Of all bad men, religious bad men are the worst."[1] Much harm has been done in the world under the banner of religious fervor and in the name of purity and holiness. But without love, it's all a clanging gong.

What if we realized through the use of our words in healthy speech, following certain communication dynamics, that we could seek and save the lost? Do we realize the power in our words to reconcile and find unity in the body of Christ?

First Corinthians 13:4–8a (ESV) says:

Love is patient and kind; love does not envy or boast; it is not arrogant or rude. It does not insist on its own way; it is not irritable or resentful; it does not rejoice at wrongdoing, but rejoices with the truth. Love bears all things, believes all things, hopes all things, endures all things.

Love never ends.

Love never ends. We think of this passage too romantically sometimes—that it's only to read at wedding ceremonies. However, this is about you and me. You and I don't dishonor each other if we love each other. We don't envy each other if we love enough to celebrate each other's successes. We aren't easily angered if we love each other enough to try to see everything from the other's perspective. We can't keep a record of wrongs if we love each other, because reconciling our relationship will be too important to us to risk it on a grudge.

Love continues to plead with God, that He would bring somebody back to us or that our relationships would be restored. To win someone. To find a lost sheep. To be found in unity with those in the church—even if we have to wage a hard peace to get there. To be reconciled.

Want to find a good church? If so, look for a church where the number one thing is that in Christ's name they understand that love never ends, and when they get it wrong, they fight to recover a posture of love—and that fight never stops.

Straight Talk

Imagine if we all carried hope into our marriages, jobs, and churches, believing the best of our coworkers, spouses, kids, friends, and fellow churchgoers. The world would be a dramatically different place, wouldn't it? We wouldn't run from difficult conversations; instead, we'd run toward them with outrageous hope that beauty and restoration would be the result. Our problem is one of grace. The one mistreated often mistreats. When we don't feel as if God has enough grace to like and accept us, we return the favor on the people we meet and miss our opportunity to hope all things.

If we have hope—if love hopes—we can still fix what comes between us. If we humbly go to the person who has wounded us, with open hands, asking questions, maybe that individual will change or we'll learn something that softens the blow. We have hope in Christ, hope in the Holy Spirit, and hope in each other. We hope things aren't always the way they appear.

We need more straight talk. Direct talk. Matter-of-fact talk. We need conversation that seeks to unify and bridge and forgive and get us to a healthy place. It's there in red letters in Matthew 18: "Just between the two of you" (v. 15). Then, "If they listen to you, you have won them over." Isn't that the whole point of all three of the parables in Matthew 18? The lost sheep that needs to be found, the sin that divides the community, and the forgiveness that must be passed on—all three are saying our aim should be to win people over and be unified.

One of the hallmarks of love is straight talk—that we hope all things. Our first reaction should be to hope all things, not to assume the worst. That means we can speak the truth because we hope confidently that the truth will be received. Our motive—even in difficult conversations—should always be to extend grace. When you're judging someone, you don't owe that person a conversation. It's too easy to put somebody into a category and feel validated in making him or her the bad person.

When it comes to the way we communicate, we always benefit from more concern and hope. If there isn't any hope or emotion, the love will grow cold quickly and come to an end. Our speech will slowly tilt toward judgment, because we love to judge and we love to punish. The law always feels good when it's a weapon in our hands working against our enemies.

We need to learn how to talk constructively to one another in our marriages, our families, and our churches. Ephesians 4:26 says, "Be angry and do not sin; do not let the sun go down on your anger" (ESV). In Romans 12:17–18, Paul writes, "Do not repay anyone evil for evil. Be careful to do what is right in the eyes of everyone. If it is possible, as far as it depends on you, live at peace with everyone." Don't play games, don't start drama, don't be in cliques, don't pass along hearsay. Paul continues in Romans 12:19, "Do not take revenge, my dear friends, but leave room for God's wrath, for it is written 'It is mine to avenge; I will repay,' says the Lord."

As a church family, we need to train our tongues for justice and righteousness. We should always be ready to gently and lovingly shut down conversation that divides, slanders, and dishonors others. We should always be steering the conversations around us toward unity and building up the family of God.

It falls to us to foster a culture in our families and church communities in which we reinforce healthy, edifying speech with one another.

The focus of Matthew 18 isn't punitive measures against sinners in our churches. It's about helping us figure out how to reconcile people—how to win over our brothers and sisters.

Our perception of God's character and the way He communicates will profoundly shape the way we speak to our family, friends, and neighbors. Knowing that Jesus sought love, unity, and relationship wherever He went leaves us with a powerful mandate to leverage our words the same way and for the same reasons.

Judgment begets judgment, but grace begets grace. And love begets love.

We have the opportunity to learn from Jesus how to bridle our tongues, bringing them into submission and training them as instruments of righteousness and restoration. Imagine that! Beautiful things can happen as we collaborate with Jesus, who promises to lead us in the peacemaking process.

Chapter 12

To Speak
a Better Word

*Laugh and fear not, creatures. Now that you are no
longer dumb and witless, you need not always be grave.
For jokes as well as justice come in with speech.*

ASLAN, *THE MAGICIAN'S NEPHEW*

In my book *Create vs. Copy*, I (Ken) explore the role
creativity plays in our participation in the reconciliation of all
things. To this end, I use the term "generous creativity" and point
to God's saving work as a form of reclamation art. God is taking
the broken things, redeeming them, and making them new.

Similarly, a look at the theology of words and speech shows us
that, in our creative work—our reclamation art—words, as much
as anything else, communicate our love and carry transforming
power to others.

Creativity, worship, justice, and words—these all make up
and inform our work as reconcilers in this world. As C. S. Lewis
wrote, "For jokes as well as justice come in with speech."

In a conversation I had with Nicholas Wolterstorff, professor emeritus at Yale, he discussed how the concepts of art, beauty, and goodness intersect with justice and education. He said:

> Art and justice, beauty and justice, are often seen as different spheres of life having little or nothing to do with each other. That's due, in part, to how we think of art. Most people, when they think of art, think of museum paintings and sculptures, concert hall music, and so forth. I have just finished the manuscript for a book that I call *Art Rethought*, in which I argue for expanding our perspective on art. I talk about memorial art, about social protest art, about work songs, and so on. In all three of these, justice lies at the very heart of that form of art. That's obviously true for social protest art. But it's also true for memorial art. The point behind a memorial is to pay honor to someone who merits such honor, to pay honor to someone for their worth or dignity is to treat them justly. And as to work songs: what strikes one in the testimony of those who sang work songs while working, especially under oppressive conditions, is that it was an expression of their human dignity; they refused to be reduced to animals. In expressing their dignity, the singers were treating themselves justly.[1]

What a concept. All the justice movements in history—from the abolitionists to the women's suffragettes, from the civil rights movement to anti-apartheid efforts in South Africa—have used words, song, and art to carry the heart of their message and to speak truth into the atmosphere of society. Words pull protesters together, and words tear down the walls of injustice.

Redeeming how we talk isn't tangential to or isolated from

this. Redeeming how we talk is directly tied to our call to join with God in the reconciliation of all things—of speaking beauty, truth, and justice into the world. Redeeming how we talk is how we turn our words from weapons into tools and our speech from mere banter into a powerful art form.

Communication as Redemptive Art

If language is one of the ways we engage in the redemption of all things, then the words we use in the different spheres of our lives take on a unique and deeply spiritual role. We can speak a better world into existence. We would like to look at some of those spheres and consider how we can use our words to strengthen relationships, build up others, and participate in God's reclamation art.

Language and Friendship

Friendship is deeply important to human well-being because it is relationship without self-interest. That is, we freely enter into friendship from a freely offered, freely received posture. We don't do it to change the other person. We don't do it to parent someone. We don't do it to pastor someone. We enter into friendship to love and be loved. Friendship, as such, is not a relationship where one assumes power *over* the other. We love each other as we are for who we are.

Ideal friendships are based on mutuality and loyalty. They have, at the center, shared interests and a common purpose, yet they maintain respect for differences that are discovered along the way. Redemptive language in friendships should take on a refining quality, so that we can offer perspective as well as encouragement and support. Proverbs 27:17 tells us that "iron sharpens iron." This requires a redemptive engagement, in which both truth and love manifest themselves in a protective environment. When we become overly concerned with controlling what the other person thinks of us, the love we have for the other person can be overshadowed, and we endanger the friendship. For friendships to fulfill their full spiritual potential, they must be collaborative rather than self-centered.

Friendship can also be a place where hard things are spoken. Proverbs 27:6 reminds us that "wounds from a friend can be trusted." Start by letting others know you welcome their input, even if it hurts at first. Honesty invited from others turns into an invitation to be honest ourselves. Knowing the power of words and how valuable the insights of friends can be, set the preconditions for transparency and resiliency in your relationships before things get difficult. Acquaintances are people we can have fun with. Friends are people with whom we've disagreed and been able to work through difficulties. If you can't trust someone with disagreement or straight talk, how can you trust them with friendship?

Language and Marriage

Marriage is the mystical union of two individuals who become one in flesh and spirit. I once heard it said that the time is right for marriage when you and your beloved can better glorify God together than you could apart. While we lose a part of our lives in marriage, it is meant to be an additive and synergistic union.

If marriage has inherently redemptive qualities, the language we use in marriage either helps to reinforce our spiritual bonds or erode them away and hollow them. Because familiarity marks every marriage, we can easily become sharper and more careless with our spouses than we are with others. Yet our spouse should be the very person we are most committed to nurturing and building up with our words.

Gary Smalley identifies five different ways couples communicate (clichés, facts, opinions, feelings, needs),[2] and they can help you identify ways to grow in your conversational habits with your spouse. Intimacy deepens as you move down the list, serving as a guide for the kinds of conversations to increase in order to strengthen your relationship.

Conversational clichés are the preprogrammed and simplified thoughts or statements we express without thinking—the kind we subliminally pick up over the years and regurgitate reflexively. They show little or no intentionality, and as such lack value. One of the most common clichés is the impenetrable "Fine" when you're asked how your day went. While perfectly normal—and it would be exhausting if every conversation was deep and intensive—conversational clichés can become conversation killers and distract you from matters of substance in life and marriage.

Like clichés, facts in conversation really only lead to intimacy if they serve as fodder for more important conversations. Talking about the weather, what's happening in the office, what the latest headlines are, any number of things related to sports trivia, and so on, often relegates us to simply trading facts and interesting tidbits. Fact-sharing avoids conflict and also veers away from anything that reveals what one thinks or feels on a deep level. Fact-sharing can become more valuable in conversation when the facts are used for transition, forming the objective bedrock that helps us get to deeper, subjective revelations and conversation.

Opinions, of course, are a step more personal. When you express an opinion, you reveal something about yourself, the way you see the world, and what you like and don't like. As such, where there are opinions, there is often conflict. Opinions expose us to differences between ourselves and others, and it can create a sense of isolation or frustration. In marriage, differing opinions can form what Smalley calls a "wall of conflict." A wall of conflict arises when something that matters to us rubs up against something that matters to our spouse. Because we are close with our spouse, these differences can feel more acute. At this point, we can choose to fight or go deeper into refining our language and understanding each other. On the other side of the wall—not necessarily agreement—is intimacy.

When we are able to get past the barriers of conflict to truly hearing one another's true voice and deepest feelings, we have moved into deep, mature, and meaningful conversation. We all want others to get us, hear us, and know our tender parts and still accept us. When we can move beyond conflict to discovery and acceptance, it frees us up to be truly vulnerable in sharing ourselves and our dreams, desires, and goals with others. We're never truly safe with another until they know and acknowledge our deep feelings and beliefs, even if they differ on opinions.

When we're sharing needs, we've moved beyond pretense and posturing. Needs are the deepest thing about us. In putting words to them, we are expressing the truest things about ourselves as emotional, relational, and spiritual beings. Additionally, in the context of need-based conversation, when one person honestly shares his or her needs and desires, the other feels safe to do likewise. When we're conversing around needs as a couple, we are at the height of generative conversation, and we're unlocking our generous creativity in each other's life.

Smalley's categories of speech show levels that begin on the surface and then move deeper. In marriage, as we evaluate how we talk to our spouse, we need to find ways to create space for deeper and more intentional dialogue so that we don't simply trade facts and a few opinions during the day, but hear and explore each other's feelings and deepest needs. One of the most important things couples can do is regularly schedule time for proactive and spiritually focused conversation, rather than give way to the reactive conversations that so easily survive amid our rushed daily patterns.

This may require flipping our priorities upside down: turning off the game, canceling ladies' night out, rescheduling dinner with the neighbors, hiring a babysitter, getting out of the house, going for a walk, planning vacations and anniversary trips, or reading the same books together for discussion. Making the time to unpack language and identify where each other is coming from in a relationship can quickly move us past misunderstandings and into healthier patterns of communication.

Language and Children

Any parent would say the well-being of their child is the most important thing they could hope for. And yet, we often fail to recognize the impact our words have on that outcome. Our words convey our concern. If we want our children to be healthy, we must nurture often, just like we water a lawn. Weeds have a much harder time growing in a lawn that is lush and healthy. How much better it is to grow health in the first place than to correct later. The words we communicate as parents are the nourishment for our kids to grow into beautiful, healthy individuals.

Even Paul, who did not have children, speaks to the importance of words in parenting—he counseled straightforwardly, "Do not exasperate your children" (Eph. 6:4). Paul understood that words spoken to a child can bring life, but they can also bring death. When we speak to our children with demeaning, demanding, and overly disciplined language, we put them in a constant position of believing they are inadequate and unworthy of our love and affection. We exasperate our children when they are always under our critical watch and the critical language that follows. Critical words smother and destroy the space in which children would otherwise have the opportunity to grow and flourish. This is why Paul gives fathers the very practical admonition not to embitter or frustrate their children. In Proverbs 18:21, King Solomon writes, "The tongue has the power of life and death." Words are a parent's best asset in trying to establish life in the hearts of their children.

Here's a challenge: counteract the negative. According to research, positive comments are more effective in productivity than constructive criticism by a ratio of nearly six positive comments to every one negative comment.[3] This certainly has a similar effect on the nurture and instruction of children. "Yes, and . . ." plays a part in this as well. Try building affirmation into your daily rhythm. Knowing when and where you will be able to bless, pray for, encourage, and build up your children will go a long way to helping you overcome the negative comments that accumulate daily in your child's life.

As parents, we should affirm their identity as children and people loved by God. We should speak the truths that we as the parent take for granted but that our children long to be reassured of.

At times, discipline is necessary, but only discipline in the context of affirmation will bring life. Putting stakes around a crooked tree doesn't come from a heart of punishment but from a spirit of redemption. In the same way, when we discipline our children, our words and tone must come from an overwhelming desire for redemption rather than to vent frustration.

Words are powerful.

In our role as parents, we should strive to identify the respective contexts in which our children feel most affirmed and loved, because it is in that context that they are best able to receive our affirmation. For example, my four daughters recently took the online version of the five love languages test. Three of them share quality time as their primary love language. Extended time allows them space to feel safe and free to be conversational. It's here where there is opportunity for intimate dialogue, lengthy conversation, and for love to be made known.

Leadership expert Michael Hyatt once wrote, "A careless word can shape—or misshape—someone's reality for years to come."[4] Prioritizing time with children is one way to make sure we speak the right words—and carefully.

Language and Influence

Like water on a rock, language over time exerts a considerable influence. What we say to others and what others say to us is deeply formative. Words and the intentions they carry form grooves in who we are. What we believe about ourselves and the world is greatly influenced by the conversations we encounter. That being true, there are ways to exert a positive influence on your community, as well as create a positive culture within which to exist yourself.

One is to avoid returning insults. In one of the strongest biblical passages that invites us to follow Jesus' example, Peter writes, "When they hurled their insults at him, he did not retaliate; when he suffered, he made no threats. Instead, he entrusted himself to him who judges justly" (1 Peter 2:23). Jesus didn't respond in kind to those who unfairly berated Him. To do so only keeps the cycle of violence going. Instead, He broke the cycle by refusing to trade insults. Proverbs 19:11 teaches us something similar: "A person's wisdom yields patience; it is to one's glory to overlook an offense." Where in your life and with which people are you trading fire or letting your feelings of victimization cause you to destroy the fabric of your community with your words? Following after Jesus, we can grow in our ability to avoid retaliation, let go of threats, and entrust ourselves to God, who judges justly on our behalf.

A second way to form a positive context for conversation is to evaluate your peer group and those influencing your speech. We pick up language from those we spend our time around, whether it's an accent, a phrase, or a tone. Proverbs 13:20 states this succinctly: "Walk with the wise and become wise, for a companion of fools suffers harm." Evaluate those with whom you spend your time. Are they helping you become the person you want to be? Or are they continually leading you back into old patterns or immature ways of talking with or about people? We can choose who we allow to shape us over time. Who could you spend more time around that would have a positive effect on you through the power of his or her words? Reach out and schedule a coffee, lunch, or movie night. And then do it again! Make it your ambition to find and surround yourself with life-giving people.

Third, practice hope. Create the habit of hope. You can never get your words back. Every word makes an impact, either for good or harm. Practice speaking words of hope. We become what we practice. Hope makes room for creativity and possibility. Hope brings life. Speaking words of good news is possibly one of the most influential ways we can speak. As Proverbs 15:30 says, "Light in a messenger's eyes brings joy to the heart, and good news gives health to the bones." Remember Nicholas Wolterstorff's thoughts on the relationship between art, poetry, song, and justice. We can indeed speak a better world into existence.

Language of Confession

There comes a time in every relationship when something challenging presents itself and the relationship is tested. Sometimes it seems as though there is no way out of the situation—no way toward healing and restoration. When in doubt, confess. That is perhaps the most important piece of advice for the restoration of relationship. If a relationship is strained, we can never start in a better place than in a posture of humble penitence. Begin with "I'm sorry" and the well of love will flow again. In some of the most famous words of the New Testament, Jesus teaches us to pray, "Forgive us our debts, as we also have forgiven our debtors" (Matt. 6:12). Interestingly, he is careful to include the converse in the next verse, "For if you forgive those who sin against you, your heavenly Father will also forgive you" (Matt. 6:14). Into the heart of His message, Jesus posits the idea that the state of our relationships with one another speaks directly to the state of our relationship with God.

One of the reasons we struggle with moving past the trials and tribulations in our lives is because we are afraid to name them. All too often, when we do name them, it is usually as an excuse or takes the form of self-pity. Our humanity, however, is built for something other than making excuses, blaming others, or simply feeling sorry for ourselves.

We are encouraged to confess our sins to one another. Most of the prayers in the Bible take on both a penitent and thankful voice despite the trials and tribulations of the person praying. Our redemptive calling is not only captured in the content of our words but also in the posture we model. I often say, "Life is messy and God is mysterious." Between these truths lives an inherent tension or anxiety. The language we use around the tension of faith, and the way our language sets an example for speaking faith into chaos and trust into confusion, is not only one of the most powerful things we can do, but it is also one of the most redemptive. Love begets love. Grace begets grace. Forgiveness begets forgiveness.

In the book of Daniel, the prophet ends a beautiful prayer, in which he exhibits no ego or self-centeredness, with the words, "We do not make requests of you because we are righteous, but because of your great mercy. Lord, listen! Lord, forgive! Lord, hear and act! For your sake, my God, do not delay, because your city and your people bear your Name" (Dan. 9:18–19).

In talking to God, Daniel is perfectly comfortable accepting the messiness of human life as something he's a part of and not distinct from. Daniel accepts the redemption of things as being God's work, not his own heroism. Making it all the more powerful, the sins Daniel confesses in his prayers are the ones committed by Israelites before he was born.

In so doing, Daniel is a picture of humility. He is the kind of person God can bless, raise up, and use. Unlike those around him in the king's court, Daniel was free from the court's tribalism and vendetta seeking and was able to be influenced by God.

There's something dangerously beautiful about a man or woman who is open and transparent enough to own his or her own faults. Anyone who is that humble and earnest has nothing to hide—and sets a good example for others. When a single person is willing to be transparent, it breaks the ice—it is the permission

Words are central to the calling of Christian faith, ministry, and witness. With words we write, preach, and teach. With words we lead, motivate, and inspire. With words we live out our vocation to love God and neighbor. **LANGUAGE IS SPIRITUAL.**

giver for others to do likewise. We all want to be known. Transparency is the path to being known.

Grace and forgiveness free us from the burden of secrecy, the deception of pride, and the stench of bitterness. They allow us to be fully human—as God intended us to be—naked in His presence and moldable as clay. Use this opportunity to ask or extend forgiveness in a relationship that has been stuck for some time. Freedom might only be a few words away.

Language of Disappointment

One of the most forgotten forms of speech in modern life is that of lament. Here in the United States—as well as in most of the Western world—we are patterned, from childhood, to be in control of and equipped to fix the problems we encounter. In an age where we can control so many aspects of our environment, when we are faced with the vicissitudes and the frailty of our human existence, we find that, for all our education, we have an underdeveloped language set regarding disappointment, pain, and suffering. There are many cultures in the world that know how to sing songs of lament and verbalize their pain in relational contexts; the Bible is rich with examples of this. But many of us are novices here.

Lamenting is different from complaining. Whereas a complaint cries "unfair," the biblical idea of lament is simply a declaration of one's pain, sometimes mixed with the cry for God or others to respond. Complaining tends to blame or criticize, but lament cries out to God for help and is usually marked with repentance and confession. Self-pity condemns God, but lamentations seek God. If reconciliation is part of the redemptive movement to restore things to the way they ought to be, then lament is how we name what is broken—that things are not as God designed them to be and that much of the fault is ours.

In one of the more extreme pictures of darkness in Scripture, the author of Psalm 74 bemoans how the Babylonian invaders of Jerusalem set up their standards over the places where God's people used to worship Him. The religious places had been stamped out in judgment against them.

The author then issues these haunting words:

> We are given no signs from God;
>> no prophets are left,
>> and none of us knows how long this will be. (Ps. 74:9)

The Psalms, which were inspired by God and became the communal prayer book of God's people (Jesus even cries out from Psalm 22 on the cross, "My God, my God, why have you forsaken me?"), not only give us permission but also supply the language of disappointment we can use with God. God coaxes us into lament as a necessary way to be fully human and deal with the disappointments and complexities of life.

The Psalms also give us a way to turn our eyes back to God in the midst of disappointment. Psalm 74 provides us with an example of this. The writer, after confessing frustration, declares what he knows to be true about God:

> But God is my King from long ago;
>> he brings salvation on the earth.
> It was you who split open the sea by your power;
>> you broke the heads of the monster in the waters.
> It was you who crushed the heads of Leviathan

and gave it as food to the creatures of the desert.
It was you who opened up springs and streams;
    you dried up the ever-flowing rivers.
The day is yours, and yours also the night;
    you established the sun and moon.
It was you who set all the boundaries of the earth;
    you made both summer and winter. (Ps. 74:12–17)

The language of disappointment, or lament, includes sharing our inner thoughts and fears. It also, for those of us seeking to live by faith, culminates in declarations of trust, affirming the qualities of God we know to be immutable and true.

It's no surprise that the language given for some of our deepest emotions comes from the Psalms—the prayer book of the Bible, *written to be sung.*

God gives us poetry for a purpose. God Himself knows that the deepest communication possible for humans comes in the form of poetry. As we reclaim the language, we engage in redemption.

Do you make a habit of pouring out your emotions to God in this way?

Language and Body

Poetic language often draws upon the body to describe what's happening in the heart, which speaks to the role of the body in communication. Posture matters. How can we use our body language redemptively?

Both of us loved watching an American TV show called *Lie to Me*, which depicted the character Dr. Cal Lightman, who was an expert in distinguishing and detecting people's facial responses and actions—what are called "microexpressions." Ultimately, his apt ability to read the minute facial and body movements of people allowed him to catch the criminal. It turns out that Dr. Lightman was a character based on an actual researcher named Dr. Paul Ekman, who demonstrated that our bodies betray the goings on in our hearts and minds even before we realize it.

Body language is what we speak with our physicality. It provides us, whether we know how to read it or not, the nuance and extra data needed to help triangulate what a person is *really* saying. What we know of a person (character and personality), what we hear (words and tone), and what we see (body language) all factor into our understanding of human communication. Body language, which includes expressive and receptive gestures, plays an instructive and corroborating role in our speech.

I'm not sure how much of a role it played in Jesus' knowledge of people's hearts, but when we are able to "read" someone, it usually comes from some degree of understanding or interpretation of his or her body language. Bodies speak and communicate all on their own.

Joe Navarro is a retired FBI special agent and an expert on nonverbal communication. A few years ago, he wrote a book called *What Every Body Is Saying*, explaining nonverbal communication and the cues we can pick up if we listen with our eyes and not just our ears. Joe was asked if body language (nonverbal communication) is distinctive to each culture or if it is universal to all people. Here's what he said:

> All behavior that comes from [the limbic system] is universal. It is hardwired; even blind children will do the same behavior having never seen it. It is found around the world. Culture

introduces nuance and other emblematic behaviors such as "OK" with a thumbs-up. So, while culture adds to the repertoire of limbic behaviors, we all have the same basic limbic reactions (fear, anger, caring, love, empathy, distrust, etc.).[5]

Body language isn't a mystical subject or secret art form; it's a part of what God designed for human communication.

Redeeming how we talk requires that we don't just pay attention to the words we use with one another. We also need to give attention to the language we speak with our bodies and, likewise, the body language of others. Go online and order a book on body language. It's possible your relationships with family, friends, work, or school will benefit tremendously from your attention to this form of communication.

The Language of Introspection

Language is a fine tool for drawing out our deepest thoughts.

Augustine of Hippo (354–430) converted to Christianity during the waning years of the Roman Empire. Coming to faith after a hedonistic youth, he is one of the towering (and most colorful) figures in church history and theology. He also holds the distinction of being the first person to write an introspective or psychological memoir, his classic *Confessions*.

Much later, but in the same vein, Michel Eyquem de Montaigne, a French skeptic who lived in the late 1500s, engaged in a series of short works in which he plumbed the depths of his psyche in an attempt to find himself through the process of self-discovery. Montaigne called his short pieces "attempts" or "trials" using the French word *essais*, popularizing what we now call "essays" as a literary genre.

Both of their efforts tell of what a deep well the human heart is. We can draw up thoughts, experiences, and inner states, and through the bizarre and holy process of communication, *turn what is personal into something relevant to others.*

But the mystery deepens: This is not necessarily a clean or even visible process. The forces that shape what and how we communicate are a unique blend, often lying deep out of sight. Often, we do not see or understand the motives driving us or our communication patterns. And this can put us at the mercy of those shadowy motives. Unless we first confront the source of our desires and motivations, our words will continue to escape us unexamined. At best, that will leave a missed opportunity to influence our world in the service of holiness and love (God's way). At worst, it will lead us to sow chaos, discord, lies, and hatred (the Serpent's way).

For both Augustine and Montaigne, their unusual vulnerability was an opportunity not only for introspection but for communication. We have the same opportunity. Communication is more than just a process of connecting two or more people through an exchange of information; it is a tool that forms our hearts and knits us together. Communicating what is truly within us demands we look inward first. Nothing is more humbling than examining the truth about ourselves.

Words are central to the calling of Christian faith, ministry, and witness. With words we write, preach, and teach. With words we lead, motivate, and inspire. With words we live out our vocation to love God and neighbor. Language is spiritual. It changes our reality and is meant to work in tandem with our actions. Forgiveness is contagious. Love rebounds. Good news spreads.

Our lives are shaped by the words we speak and the words spoken over us. Sometimes we become the words of creative goodness. And, sometimes, we digress into the words of destructive enmity. This underscores the ever-important responsibility we have in speaking words over others. Our words can curse or they can bless.

Our words are alive. Our very being is language. With our words, we hold the power to reclaim, redeem, and reconcile. How we communicate might be one of the most sacred art forms there is, and redeeming how we talk might be one of the most important steps of growth we can take.

Blessed Words

Words are all we have.

SAMUEL BECKETT

Throughout this book we have been asserting that there is a deep spirituality to words.

Words can come from God: "The LORD reached out his hand and touched my mouth and said to me, 'I have put my words in your mouth'" (Jer. 1:9). Words form a central part of our worship: "May these words of my mouth and this meditation of my heart be pleasing in your sight, LORD, my Rock and my Redeemer" (Ps. 19:14). And words—or speech—emanate from all creation testifying to the nature of God: "The heavens declare the glory of God. . . . Day after day they pour forth speech" (Ps. 19:1–2). Jesus said that even if the crowds were silent, "the very stones would cry out" (Luke 19:40 ESV).

Peter speaks to the formation of our spiritual and corporate identities when he says to many Christians all throughout Galatia, "You are a chosen people, a royal priesthood, a holy nation, God's special possession, that you *may declare* the praises of him who called you out of darkness into his wonderful light" (1 Peter 2:9).

It can be said that the aim of *all* creation is speech, both animate and inanimate creation. The trees and the mountains and the seas. The birds of the air, the fish of the sea, everything that creeps on dry land. The people—men and women—who sit within the days of creation, as stewards, and in relationship with creation and its Creator. All of creation has as its end the manifestation of words, of speech, of praise in harmonious concert back to God.

All of creation is in dialogue. All of creation speaks.

The Eucharist

There is something deeply primal and spiritual about speech and communication that flows freely from the creative activity of God. Our words have the capacity to carry with them what is good, true, and beautiful. Our words do more than relay information; they can truly pull us closer to God. Likewise, God uses His Word and the message planted in us to draw us closer to Himself.

One of the most gracious gifts Jesus has given His church is an image—that of bread and wine, a physical representation of His presence in the world. Two of the historically recognized means of grace within Christianity are the preaching of God's Word and the Lord's Supper, or Eucharist. In preaching, the good news of God's already-present and still-to-come kingdom is made audible. In the Eucharist, it is made visible. The good news is encapsulated in a regular ritual practice that renews and reenergizes our understanding of the gospel. It is not only visible, but it also appeals to all five of our senses. We can see, touch, taste, and smell the bread and wine, and often we hear the associated Scripture as we partake. It is a concrete image. As pastors, we frequently remind our congregations that Communion is not a metaphor; we are actually invited to commune with the Father, Son, and Spirit as we come to the table.

And we don't *take* Communion, as if we had to pry God's grace out of His clenched fist. We *receive* it, as a gift. He freely offers us the grace of Christ's body and blood in bread (the food of peasants) and wine (the drink of kings). At the Lord's Table, we all—janitors and judges, ex-prostitutes and PhDs, convicts and CEOs—eat from the same loaf and drink of the same cup. We celebrate our oneness with Christ and our oneness with one another. At the table, we both receive and extend forgiveness, acceptance, and love.

I believe it was Karl Barth who once said something like, "The church doesn't have an opinion; it has a view of the cross." In a very real sense, when you start where the world is, you start with an opinion. The Eucharist, or Communion, is the opposite. At the table, we start with reality. Theologian Miroslav Volf sums it up well:

> When God sets out to embrace the enemy, the result is the cross.... Having been embraced by God, we must make space for others in ourselves and invite them in—even our enemies. This is what we enact as we celebrate the Eucharist. In receiving Christ's broken body and spilled blood, we, in a sense, receive all those whom Christ received by suffering.[1]

At its core, the ultimate goal of communication is the same as this Eucharist—or Communion. The goal is a "common union" between souls and with the living God. This is what is pictured in the Eucharist. We enter a conversation. We enter the retelling of God's provision and blessing for us in Christ Jesus.

The book of Hebrews begins with these encouraging words that sum up much of the heart of this book:

> In the past God spoke to our ancestors through the prophets at many times and in various ways, but in these last days he has spoken to us by his Son, whom he appointed heir of all things, and through whom also he made the universe. The Son is the radiance of God's glory and the exact representation of his being, *sustaining all things by his powerful word.* (Heb. 1:1–3)

The words of the gospel are the same to us all. You are loved. God speaks His love over you. Every day. From eternity to eternity. Receive His words. For it is only in hearing and receiving that our world will heal. The word has been spoken. Do you hear it?

Benediction

At the Last Supper, Jesus spoke some of His last and most meaningful words. The truth is, last words matter. They matter the way a conclusion matters. The final word is the remembered word. I (A. J.) still remember the last words I received from my grandfather. They were in a birthday note he sent to me. He had put the birthday card in the mailbox just an hour before having a massive heart attack and leaving this world. His last words in the letter: "I love you, grandson. Stay healthy."

In Numbers 6, God gives the pattern for the priestly blessing—the words of blessing that the priests in the Old Testament of God were supposed to regularly speak over the people to define and reinforce their identity as God's chosen people. It was what concluded their assembly. It was what they would regularly hear as last words. As such, it was a blessing well known to the people of Israel. Much like the Lord's Prayer today, it was so familiar that people could recite it upon hearing the first few words. It goes like this:

> The LORD said to Moses, "Tell Aaron and his sons, 'This is how you are to bless the Israelites. Say to them:
> """The LORD bless you
>   and keep you;
> the LORD make his face shine on you
>   and be gracious to you;
> the LORD turn his face toward you
>   and give you peace."'

> "So they will put my name on the Israelites, and I will bless them." (vv. 22–27)

We can see this blessing in practice when Aaron, in Leviticus 9:22, "lifted his hands toward the people and blessed them. And having sacrificed the sin offering, the burnt offering and the fellowship offering, he stepped down."

Hands were raised, a blessing was given, and then he descended from the high place.

Many have speculated that this blessing is what Jesus would have given before ascending into heaven. Luke 24 recounts the story:

> When he had led them out to the vicinity of Bethany, he lifted up his hands and blessed them. While he was blessing them, he left them and was taken up into heaven. Then they

worshiped him and returned to Jerusalem with great joy. And they stayed continually at the temple, praising God. (Luke 24:50–53)

Jesus raised His arms. Then, He offered a blessing that was familiar to His audience. It is very likely they were reciting the words in their hearts as their lips mumbled them. But this time it's different. This time it's grounded in the fact of the resurrection and the knowledge that Jesus came to fully represent God as His word to creation. This time the words of blessing have additional power—they undergird the identity of His followers in a new and fuller way.

Jesus speaks His last words. He goes up, but His disciples come down from the mountain—with great joy and songs of praise on their lips.

In some respect, we've lost the full spiritual sense of prayers of blessing. We no longer remember or recite the words God gave the priests to speak over His people. Maybe we're in need of more of these words, words of benediction. Accordingly, at the end of every church service (at Theopholis) we speak a benediction—literally, "good words"—over the church.

Final words.

Grounding words.

Benedictions have been used in the history of the church as concluding words spoken or prayed over the church to go, be, and follow Jesus in His grace and mercy. They are words to remind us that we are not just recipients of the good news, but also tellers of it. It is perhaps the best part of the service. In fact, many of the doxology texts, prayers or praises in the New Testament letters, have been used as benedictions.

We are connected with God through the Word. We are connected to others through words.

When the dark side of our humanity grabs us as part of our human and competitive striving, we play with the strings of spoken words in the world. When the peace of God is settled in us, our words have a rhythm and tone, and they reinforce the love of God.

Words are ubiquitous, and they are inextricably spiritual. Words are extensions of every heart, and they carry the force of every human will in this world.

And, ultimately, words will shape not only us but the world around us.

"Through the blessing of the upright a city is exalted" (Prov. 11:11).

Acknowledgments

I, Ken, would like to thank all those who have been gracious and patient through the process these last years of working out my thoughts through writing. In these times I realize how important the love of friends and family truly is.

Thank you to Tamara, as always, for seeing the best in me. And thank you to Rick Gerhardt for the beauty of long-term friendship and collaboration.

To Kip Jones—much of what you have done over the years has allowed me to do what I have done. Thank you.

Thank you also to Rachel Goble and Alexia Salvatierra for important phone calls and conversations at the outset of this project.

Thank you to Antioch Church for allowing me the space to learn and write.

I would like to thank Adrianne Salmond, Marie Teilhard, Linda Van Voorst, and Bill Buck for helpful editorial reads.

Adrianne Salmond contributed numerous edits and substantial help with citations. Pete Kelley graciously helped with thoughts on the Eucharist.

Thank you to Steve Janney, who taught me a lot about direct speech and tackling things head-on in my formative ministry years.

Finally, to my mom, who gave me the love of words, and to my youngest daughter, Ashlin, who carries on the tradition. To my other daughters: Mary Joy, who reads words; Esther, who sings them; and Sara, who writes them. You are my joy.

I, A. J., wish to first thank my family. Elliot, you have been generous and patient with me as I've either sat at the computer or in the reading chair, doing my work on this project. I owe you the best dim sum lunch you could dream of. And for my beautiful bride, Quinn. Your beauty and your wit are matched only by your deep love of God, and I am proud to have given you my last name.

For Theophilus, the church I pastor. You are a mystery. And I wonder how we are still one. But you are a miracle. For in all our disagreements, tears, toils, and struggles, we have learned to still find our life in the power of the bread and the cup. Jesus makes us a miracle. And without Him, we'd have been done years ago.

I wish to thank Trevor Gavin for giving me the iPad he didn't want anymore. I wish you had left the Kindle books on there, but I am glad to have received the device nonetheless.

Finally, to my parents: I praise God for you.

We both would like to thank the team at Moody Publishers, Ingrid Beck, and Matthew Boffey for their endurance, creativity, and belief in us.

To Don Jacobson and those at D. C. Jacobson, thank you for the continued support.

Notes

Introduction: When Language Gets Lost

1. Tad Friend, "Jumpers: The Fatal Grandeur of the Golden Gate Bridge," *New Yorker*, October 13, 2013, https://www.newyorker.com/magazine/2003/10/13/jumpers.
2. The title and theme of Sherry Turkle's brilliant watershed book *Alone Together: Why We Expect More from Technology and Less from Each Other* (New York: Basic Books, 2012).
3. Maia Szalavitz, "Touching Empathy: Lack of Physical Affection Can Actually Kill Babies," *Psychology Today*, March 1, 2010, https://www.psychologytoday.com/blog/born-love/201003/touching-empathy.
4. Aaron Kheriaty, "Dying of Despair," *First Things*, August 2017, https://www.firstthings.com/article/2017/08/dying-of-despair.
5. "Few Clinton or Trump Supporters Have Close Friends in the Other Camp: How Voters Are Talking—or Arguing—about the Campaign," Pew Research Center, August 3, 2016, http://www.people-press.org/2016/08/03/few-clinton-or-trump-supporters-have-close-friends-in-the-other-camp/.
6. Os Guinness, *Prophetic Untimeliness: A Challenge to the Idol of Relevance* (Ada, MI: Baker, 2003), 17.

Chapter 1: A Creative Word

1. Although, it is interesting that in Genesis 2, God does make Adam out of the dust of the ground. Whether or not He used His hands to do so is up for great debate; but God made humans out of that which already existed—dust. Thus, humans are derivative of what God spoke into existence.
2. Brian Greene, *The Elegant Universe: Superstrings, Hidden Dimensions, and the Quest for the Ultimate Theory* (New York: W. W. Norton, 2003), 15–16.
3. For a more extended treatment and quotations, see Ken Wytsma's *Create vs. Copy: Embrace Change. Ignite Creativity. Break Through with Imagination.*
4. Colin E. Gunton, *The Christian Faith: An Introduction to Christian Doctrine* (Oxford: Blackwell, 2002), 5; Francis Watson, *Text, Church and World: Biblical Interpretation in Theological Perspective* (Edinburgh: T&T Clark, 1994), 142–43.
5. Dietrich Bonhoeffer, "What Is Meant by 'Telling the Truth'?" in *Ethics*, ed. Eberhard Bethge, trans. Neville Horton Smith (New York: Touchstone, 1955), 361.
6. Karl Barth, *Letters 1961–1968*, trans. Geoffrey W. Bromley (Grand Rapids, MI: Eerdmans, 1981), 284.
7. William H. Willimon, "Formed by the Saints," *Christian Century* 113, no. 5 (February 7–14, 1996): 136–37.

Chapter 2: Propaganda

1. Tacitus, *Annals, Book XV.*
2. Tim Wu, *The Attention Merchants: The Epic Scramble to Get Inside our Heads* (New York: Alfred E. Knopf, 2016), 39.
3. Wu, *Attention Merchants,* 38.
4. Wu, *Attention Merchants,* 43.
5. Wu, *Attention Merchants,* 45.
6. *American Experience: The Great War, A Nation Comes of Age,* part 2, directed by Amanda Pollak, written by Stephen Ives, featuring Christopher Capozzola, aired April 12, 2017, on PBS, http://www.pbs.org/wgbh/americanexperience/films/great-war/.
7. Wu, *Attention Merchants,* 50.
8. *English Oxford Living Dictionaries,* s.v. "propaganda," accessed February 1, 2017, https://en.oxforddictionaries.com/definition/propaganda.
9. Jason Stanley, *How Propaganda Works* (Princeton, NJ: Princeton University Press, 2015), 12.
10. Wu, *Attention Merchants,* 6.
11. Henry David Thoreau, *Life without Principle* (Heraklion, 1863), chap. 1, Kindle.
12. Matthew B. Crawford, *The World Beyond Your Head: On Becoming an Individual in an Age of Distraction* (New York: Farrar, Straus and Giroux, 2015), 13.
13. Thoreau, *Life without Principle,* chap. 1.
14. Walter Brueggemann, "The Sabbath as Resistance: An interview with Walter Brueggemann," interview by Ken Wytsma, http://kenwytsma.com/2014/10/20/sabbath-as-resistance-an-interview-with-walter-brueggemann.
15. Brueggemann, "Sabbath as Resistance."
16. Wendell Berry (@WendellDaily), "It is not from ourselves that we learn to be better than we are," Twitter, Oct 15, 2016, 6:02 a.m., https://twitter.com/wendelldaily/status/787277471003643904.
17. Leroy Barber, conversation with Ken Wytsma, December 21, 2017.
18. Robert Ellsberg, ed., *Dorothy Day: Selected Writings* (Maryknoll, NY: Orbis, 2001), 106.
19. Stanley, *How Propaganda Works,* 12.

Chapter 3: The Challenge of Connecting in a Digital Age

1. Judith Burns, "Parents' Mobile Use Harms Family Life, Say Secondary Pupils," BBC News, April 23, 2017, http://www.bbc.com/news/education-39666863.
2. Jean M. Twenge, "Have Smartphones Destroyed a Generation?" *The Atlantic,* September 2017, https://www.theatlantic.com/magazine/archive/2017/09/has-the-smartphone-destroyed-a-generation/534198/.
3. Twenge, "Smartphones."

4. Twenge, "Smartphones."

5. Susan Weinschenk, PhD, "Why We're All Addicted to Texts, Twitter and Google: Dopamine Makes You Addicted to Seeking Information in an Endless Loop," *Psychology Today*, September 11, 2012, https://www.psychologytoday.com/blog/brain-wise/201209/why-were-all-addicted-texts-twitter-and-google.

6. James Vincent, "Former Facebook Exec Says Social Media Is Ripping Apart Society," The Verge, December 11, 2017, https://www.theverge.com/2017/12/11/16761016/former-facebook-exec-ripping-apart-society.

7. Vincent, "Former Facebook Exec."

8. Max Frisch, *Homer Faber*, trans. Michael Bullock (Orlando, FL: Harcourt, 1959), 178.

9. Carl F. H. Henry, *God, Revelation, and Authority*, vol. 1, *God Who Speaks and Shows: Preliminary Considerations* (Wheaton, IL: Crossway, 1999), 30.

10. Stanley Hauerwas, as quoted in William Willimon, *Pastor: The Theology and Practice of Ordained Ministry* (Nashville: Abingdon Press, 2002), 60.

11. Brenton Dickieson, "A Statistical Look at C. S. Lewis' Letter Writing," *A Pilgrim in Narnia* (blog), May 23, 2013, https://apilgriminnarnia.com/2013/05/23/statistical-letter-writing/.

12. Martin Heidegger, *Poetry, Language, Thought*, trans. Albert Hofstadter (New York: Perennial Classics, 2001), 163.

Chapter 4: A Brief History of Information

1. "The History of Communication," History World, http://www.historyworld.net/wrldhis/PlainTextHistories.asp?historyid=aa93.

2. "Industrial Age," *World Heritage Encyclopedia*, Nook eBook Library, http://www.nook-library.com/articles/eng/industrial_age.

3. In 1965, Intel cofounder Gordon Moore observed that the number of transistors per square inch on an integrated circuit had doubled every year since their invention. He predicted this trend would continue, and thus was born "Moore's Law." In 2016, both the *MIT Technology Review* and *Nature: International Weekly Journal of Science* stated that Moore's Law is slowing down. The MIT article also said that Intel had predicted silicon chips will only continue shrinking for another five years. Tom Simonite, "Moore's Law Is Dead. Now What?" *MIT Technology Review*, May 13, 2016, https://www.technologyreview.com/s/601441/moores-law-is-dead-now-what/. M. Mitchell Waldrop, "The Chips Are Down for Moore's Law," February 9, 2016, https://www.nature.com/news/the-chips-are-down-for-moore-s-law-1.19338.

4. "The Agenda with Steve Paikin," YouTube video, 25:16, July 6, 2011, posted by James Gleick, https://www.youtube.com/watch?v=iiA7XEI20GY.

5. "Figure 5-1: Content Growth Drives Innovation," Webreference, September 23, 2002, http://www.webreference.com/authoring/design/information/iawww/chap5/1/index.html.

6. Bernard J. Luskin, EdD, LMFT, "Brain Behavior and Media: Is Media Influencing Your Brain and Your Behavior through Psychology?" *Psychology Today*, March 29, 2012, https://www.psychologytoday.com/blog/the-media-psychology-effect/201203/brain-behavior-and-media.

7. Luskin, "Brain Behavior and Media."

8. Luskin, "Brain Behavior and Media."

9. Daniel J. Levitin, *The Organized Mind: Thinking Straight in the Age of Information Overload* (New York: Plume, 2015), 308–10.

10. James Gleick, "How Google Dominates Us," *The New York Review of Books*, Aug. 18, 2011. Http://www.nybooks.com/articles/2011/08/18/how-google-dominates-us/.

11. For more information, consider watching *Denial*, a 2016 movie based on Deborah Lipstadt's book *History on Trial*, http://www.imdb.com/title/tt4645330/.

12. Deborah Lipstadt, "Behind the Lies of Holocaust Denial," filmed April 2017 at TEDxSkoll, TED video, 0:27, https://www.ted.com/talks/deborah_lipstadt_behind_the_lies_of_holocaust_denial.

13. Lipstadt, "Behind the Lies."

14. Ralph Keyes, "The Post-Truth Era: Dishonesty and Deception in Contemporary Life," ralphkeyes.com, http://www.ralphkeyes.com/the-post-truth-era/.

15. Keyes, "The Post-Truth Era."

16. C. S. Lewis, *Studies in Words* (Cambridge, UK: Cambridge University Press, 1960), 7–8.

17. George Bernard Shaw, *Ireland Calling* (blog), http://ireland-calling.com/george-bernard-shaw-quotes-the-arts/.

18. Lipstadt, "Behind the Lies," TED video, 3:40, 5:20.

Chapter 5: Here Be Dragons

1. New World Encyclopedia, s.v. "Seneca," accessed February 3, 2018, http://www.newworldencyclopedia.org/entry/Seneca.

2. "Anglo-Saxon Mappa Mundi, 1025–1050," British Library, March 26, 2009, http://www.bl.uk/onlinegallery/onlineex/unvbrit/a/001cottibb00005u00056v00.html.

3. For additional analysis of the Social Gospel Movement or issues of justice in society, see *Pursuing Justice: The Call to Live and Die for Bigger Things* and *The Myth of Equality: Uncovering the Roots of Injustice and Privilege*, both by Ken Wytsma.

4. Warren Hamilton Lewis, *Brothers and Friends: The Diaries of Major Warren Hamilton Lewis*, ed. Clyde S. Kilby and Marjorie Lamp Mead (New York: Harper & Row, 1983), 34.

5. Bill Bishop, *The Big Sort: Why the Clustering of Like-Minded America Is Tearing Us Apart* (New York: Mariner Books, 2009).

6. William Barclay, "A Comparison of Paul's Missionary Method and Preaching to the Church," in *Apostolic History and the Gospel: Biblical and Historical Essays Presented to F. F. Bruce* (Exeter, UK: The Paternoster Press, 1970), 165–66.

7. Barclay, "A Comparison," 165–66.

8. "'Kill the Indian, and Save the Man': Capt. Richard H. Pratt on the Education of Native Americans," History Matters: The U.S. Survey Course on the Web, http://historymatters.gmu.edu/d/4929/.

9. Kelly Leonard and Tom Yorton, *Yes, And: How Improvisation Reverses "No, But" Thinking and Improves Creativity and Collaboration* (New York: HarperCollins, 2015), 198.

10. Leonard and Yorton, *Yes, And*, 29.

11. Dietrich Bonhoeffer, *Life Together: The Classic Exploration of Faith in Community*, trans. John W. Doberstein (San Francisco: HarperSanFrancisco, 1954), 17.

12. Bonhoeffer, *Life Together*, 17–18.

Chapter 6: Jesus Speaks

1. Archibald MacLeish, quoted by Dr. George Sheehan in *Running & Being: The Total Experience* (New York: Rodale, 2013), 246.

2. N. T. Wright, *Reflecting the Glory: Meditations for Living Christ's Life in the World* (Minneapolis, MN: Augsburg Books, 1998), 87.

3. Saint Augustine, *Essential Sermons*, ed. Boniface Ramsey, trans. Edmund Hill (New York: New City Press, 2007), 197.

4. James W. Robinson and John B. Cobb Jr., eds., *New Frontiers in Theology: The New Hermeneutic*, vol. 2 (New York: Harper & Row, 1964), 61.

5. Kenneth J. Collins, *A Real Christian: The Life of John Wesley* (Nashville: Abingdon Press, 1999), 95.

6. C. S. Lewis, *Reflections on the Psalms* (San Diego: Harcourt, 1986), 5.

7. Dallas Willard, *The Spirit of the Disciplines: Understanding How God Changes Lives* (New York: HarperCollins, 1998), 3–4.

8. Thomas Merton, *No Man Is an Island* (Boston: Shambhala, 2005), 134.

9. Eugene H. Peterson, *Earth and Altar: The Community of Prayer in a Self-Bound Society* (Downers Grove, IL: InterVarsity Press, 1985), 86.

Chapter 7: What Is Godly Speech?

1. Thomas Merton, *The Living Bread* (New York: Farrar, Straus and Giroux, 1956), xiii.

2. Ronald Rolheiser, "About Ron," RonRolheiser.com, http://ronrolheiser.com/about-ron/, accessed January 23, 2018.

3. Dietrich Bonhoeffer, *Life Together: The Classic Exploration of Faith in Community*, trans. John W. Doberstein (San Francisco: HarperSanFrancisco, 1954), 35.

4. Henri J. M. Nouwen, *Reaching Out: The Three Movements of the Spiritual Life* (New York: Doubleday, 1966), 43–44.

5. Nouwen, *Reaching Out*, 34.

6. Bonhoeffer, *Life Together*, 23–24.

Chapter 8: On Wisdom and Words

1. Helmut Thielicke, *A Little Exercise for Young Theologians* (Grand Rapids, MI: Eerdmans, 1962).

Chapter 9: The Mechanics of Hearing One Another

1. Uri Hasson, "This Is Your brain on Communication," ideas.TED.com, January 27, 2017, https://ideas.ted.com/this-is-your-brain-on-communication/.

2. C. S. Lewis, *The Four Loves* (New York: Harcourt Brace, 1960), 65.

3. Nadia Whitehead, "People Would Rather Be Electrically Shocked Than Left Alone with Their Thoughts," *Science*, July 3, 2014, http://www.sciencemag.org/news/2014/07people-would-rather-be-electrically-shocked-left-alone-their-thoughts.

4. Kelly Leonard and Tom Yorton, *Yes, And: How Improvisation Reverses "No, But" Thinking and Improves Creativity and Collaboration* (New York: HarperCollins, 2015), 198.

5. Alexia Salvatierra, conversation with Ken Wytsma, April 19, 2017.

6. As we prepared to write this chapter, we asked our friends Stephan and Belinda Bauman to recommend a couple of books specific to cross-cultural understanding in international contexts. Stephan, the former president of World Relief, and Belinda, a leader of a movement of women fighting global injustice centered on gender violence, both hold this subject near and dear to their hearts. They recommended *Figuring Foreigners Out: A Practical Guide*, by Craig Storti, and *Cross-Cultural Conflict: Building Relationships for Effective Ministry*, by Duane Elmer.

7. Quoting Duane Elmer, *Cross-Cultural Conflict: Building Relationships for Effective Ministry* (Downers Grove, IL: InterVarsity Press, 1993), 13.

8. Elmer, *Cross-Cultural Conflict*, 13–14.

Chapter 10: The Unity of the Church

1. Philip Slater, "Connected We Stand: Are Progressives Missing the Chance to Capitalize on a Major Cultural Transformation?," *UTNE Reader*, March/April 2003, http://www.utne.com/community/connected-we-stand.

2. The thesis of Robert J. Banks's book *Paul's Idea of Community: The Early House Churches in Their Cultural Setting*.

3. Roger E. Olson, *The Mosaic of Christian Belief: Twenty Centuries of Unity and Diversity*, 2nd ed. (Downers Grove, IL: InterVarsity Press, 2002), 289.

4. *Theological Dictionary of the New Testament*, vol. 3, ed. Gerhard Kittel, trans. Geoffrey Bromiley (Grand Rapids, MI: Eerdmans, 1965), 396.

5. Eugene H. Peterson, *Tell It Slant: A Conversation on the Language of Jesus in His Stories and Prayers* (Grand Rapids, MI: Eerdmans, 2008), 28.

6. Peterson, *Tell It Slant*.

7. Robert Wuthnow, *Sharing the Journey: Support Groups and the Quest for a New Community* (New York: The Free Press, 1994).

8. "Panem et Circenses," Capitoleum.org, http://www.capitoleum.org/eng/imperatori/circenses.htm.

9. Stanley Hauerwas, "Conflict vs Comfort," in *Sunday Asylum with Stanley Hauerwas*, video 0.35, http://www.theworkofthepeople.com/conflict-vs-comfort.

10. C. S. Lewis, *The Four Loves* (New York: Harcourt Brace, 1960), 155–56.

Chapter 11: The Art of Winning People Back

1. C. S. Lewis, *Reflections on the Psalms* (Boston: Houghton Mifflin Harcourt, 1958), 32.

Chapter 12: To Speak a Better Word

1. Nicholas Wolterstorff, "Nicholas Wolterstorff on Justice, Art, Love & Human Flourishing," interview by Ken Wytsma, Theology and Culture, February 24, 2015, http://kenwytsma.com/2015/02/24/re-post-nicholas-wolterstorff-on-justice-art-love-human-flourishing/.

2. Gary Smalley, *Secrets to Lasting Love: Uncovering the Keys to Life-Long Intimacy* (New York: Fireside, 2001), 240–41.

3. Jack Zenger and Joseph Folkman, "The Ideal Praise-to-Criticism Ratio," *Harvard Business Review*, March 15, 2013, https://hbr.org/2013/03/the-ideal-praise-to-criticism.

4. Michael Hyatt, "How Our Words Impact Others: Harnessing the Power of the Tongue," *Michael Hyatt* (blog), July 22, 2016, https://michaelhyatt.com/how-our-words-impact-others/.

5. Email correspondence between Adrianne Salmond and Joe Navarro, March 30, 2017.

Conclusion: Blessed Words

1. Miroslav Volf, *Exclusion and Embrace: A Theological Exploration of Identity, Otherness, and Reconciliation* (Nashville: Abingdon Press, 1996), 129.

About the Authors

A. J. Swoboda

Dr. A. J. Swoboda is a professor, author, and pastor of Theophilus Church in urban Portland, Oregon. He is the lead mentor of a Doctor of Ministry program on the Holy Spirit and Leadership at Fuller Seminary, and teaches theology, biblical studies, and Christian history at a number of other universities and Bible colleges. He is the director of Blessed Earth Northwest, an organization focused on creation care issues and Sabbath in the Pacific Northwest. A. J. also serves as the executive director of the Seminary Stewardship Alliance—a consortium of Christian higher-ed schools that provide Christian training in creation care and are implementing sustainable practices. Previous to this, A. J. served as a campus pastor at the University of Oregon. His doctoral research at the University of Birmingham (U.K.) explored the never-ending relationship between the Holy Spirit and ecology. A. J. is also the curator of www.greenjesus.com, a site on creation care. He is the author of *Subversive Sabbath*, *The Dusty Ones*, *Tongues and Trees: Toward a Pentecostal Ecological Theology*, and *Introducing Evangelical Ecotheology*. You can find him at his website and blog at www.ajswoboda.com, or follow him on Twitter @mrajswoboda.

Ken Wytsma

Ken Wytsma is a leader, innovator, and social entrepreneur. His work takes him around the world as a frequent international speaker on justice, theology, and leadership. Ken is known for his depth of insight and ability to inspire others to think deeply about faith, life, and leadership. Ken is the lead pastor of Village Church in Beaverton, Oregon—a multicultural community in Christ. He is also the founder of The Justice Conference, which has reached over thirty thousand people across seven countries with a message on a theology of justice and God's call to give our lives away, and the founder of Kilns College, where he teaches courses on philosophy and justice. Ken is the author of *Pursuing Justice*, *The Grand Paradox*, *Create vs. Copy*, and *The Myth of Equality*, recently named as one of the top five Religion books of 2017 by *Publishers Weekly*. He has written widely, with articles appearing in *RELEVANT* Magazine, *Huffington Post*, Church Leaders, *Outreach* magazine, *Worship Leader* magazine, and more. Ken lives in Portland, Oregon, with his wife, Tamara, and their four daughters. For speaking requests or to find out more, visit kenwytsma.com.

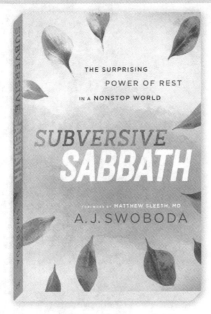
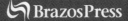